Letters to Jess & Kate

Letters to Jess & Kate

James Cantelon

THOMAS NELSON
PUBLISHERS
Nashville

Published in Nashville, Tennessee, by Thomas Nelson, Inc., Publishers,
and distributed in Canada by Word Communications, Inc., Richmond,
British Columbia.

Library of Congress Cataloging-in-Publication Data
Cantelon, James.
    Letters to Jess & Kate / James Cantelon.
        p.   cm.
    ISBN 0-8407-9684-6 (pbk.)
    1. Cantelon, James—Correspondence. 2. Uncles—Correspondence.
3. Children of divorced parents—Correspondence. 4. Divorce.
I. Title. II Title: Letters to Jess and Kate.
HQ814C34   1994
308.87—dc20   93-42907
                                                                  CIP

Printed in the United States of America.
1 2 3 4 5 6 — 99 98 97 96 95 94

1

Dear Jess and Kate,

Hi! How are you? Aunt Jenny and I are thinking about you today. We think you are probably feeling sad about your parents' divorce. So are we. Divorce is sad. It never makes you feel good.

I know this because your mom and I went through an experience like yours when we were about your age. Your mom was eight and I was ten—and you, Jess, are eleven, and Kate, you're nine, right? I phoned your mom last night and she said it was okay to tell you this story—so, here goes!

It was Christmas Eve in Butte, Montana. Snow had been falling for three days, and that night it was blowing with a strong east wind. Our little two-bedroom house was shuddering with the gusts of driving snow—in fact, I remember how our bedroom window would shake in the wind and a fine snow dust would somehow find its way through the unseen gaps around the window frame. My bed was right under the window; your mom's was on the other side of the room. Sometimes after a storm like that she and I would draw pictures in the snow covering my bedspread.

Your mom and I had been growing very close that year. We didn't notice it at the time; but in looking back, we have often remembered that year as the time we really began to love each other. Now, we still had our brother-sister arguments, but I remember feeling more protective about her. I think I know today why I felt that way, but at the time I didn't even think about it.

Dad came home drunk that night. Your mom and I had just finished decorating the tree when the back door slammed and Dad roared in. Without Mother even telling us, your mom and I quickly went to our bedroom—we had gone there a lot that year. For almost an hour we heard Dad shouting at Mother. We overheard much of what he said. He was yelling at her about the price of Christmas presents, and he said something that stuck with me for the rest of my childhood. "Those kids aren't worth twenty dollars each!" he roared. "In fact, they're nothing but trouble. I wish we'd never had them!" I cradled your mom in my arms and she cried.

Christmas morning was kind of sad. We liked our presents all right, but Dad didn't bother to get up, and I saw Mother brushing tears from her eyes several times. Two days later Dad left us. Said he was going south to warmer weather. We never saw him again. We were told only recently that he died a few years later and was buried in an unmarked grave in Mexico.

So why am I telling you this sad story? Here's why. Do you know how I felt about Dad leaving us? Sad, yes. But I also felt that his leaving was my fault. In fact, I felt that his drinking and his fighting with Mother were my fault too.

I would sometimes lie under the covers of my bed thinking that if I hadn't been born, or if I were just a better boy, my parents would be happy. And when Dad left, I felt like he was rejecting me because I was no good and I deserved this unhappiness. It was all my fault. At least, that's how I felt. Do you think it was all my fault?

It wasn't until four years later, in my first year in high school, that I began to to understand whose fault it really was. My football coach showed me that Dad's decision to leave was *Dad's* decision. He did what he did because he wanted to please himself. And yet, in some sad sort of way, Dad could never really please himself. He was in constant pain. Not physical pain like a toothache, but emotional and spiritual pain like a heartache.

Anybody who drinks heavily is trying to escape pain. Dad had a heartache that began when he was a boy; he was beaten regularly by his drunken father. He grew up hating himself. He married Mother, but could never really believe she loved him. Mother *did* love him, but he had never felt loved as a child and for some reason couldn't feel loved as an adult. He felt like a loser—and expected to fail in anything he did.

So Dad "pleased" himself by escape. He dulled the pain with alcohol, but the pain always came back. His pain would never go away until he chose to see himself as lovable, good, and dependable. But he wouldn't. Sadly, he never admitted he had a problem, never asked for help, and finally chose to run from his wife and kids. We weren't the problem. *He* was the problem.

Now, I know the circumstances in your story are not necessarily the same. But one thing *is* the same. Your dad has gone. His place at the breakfast table is empty. There's no deep male voice around the house. I want you to know that it's not your fault that he left. It's right to feel sad. It's right to cry about it. It's right even to feel angry about it. But it's not right to feel guilty about it. It's *not* your fault.

I have a question. Would you, Jess and Kate, be interested in letting me write you every week? There's a lot I would like to talk with you about in letters. I'm not saying you've got to write *me* every week! You've got homework and all kinds of other stuff on your mind, although I would like to hear from you occasionally. But I'd love to write you—if you give me permission!

Aunt Jenny and I love you very much. We're sorry we live so far away, but we're thinking of you every day and praying for you. Say hi to your mom!

Love you!
Uncle Bob

2⎯⎯⎯⎯⎯⎯⎯⎯⎯⎯⎯

Dear Jess and Kate,

Thanks for your letters. Aunt Jenny and I are so pleased that you would like us to write you each week. I want you to know that every Thursday is write-Jess-and-Kate-day. And the letter will be in the mail every Friday morning—which means, I hope, that you should get a letter every Monday or Tuesday. You can count on it.

Aunt Jenny reminded me last week that there are some things about your mom's and my childhood that are not like yours at all. For example, our dad left us and never returned, leaving Mother without divorcing her. In your case, however, you will get to see your dad from time to time, even though he lives far away. But one thing is the same for you as it was for your mom and me—your dad is gone and you're going to miss him. I know how that feels. Let me tell you a story.

That Christmas Eve storm I told you about in my last letter didn't quit for at least two weeks. It blew and blew, and the snow on the ground grew and grew. Because of the fierce wind and huge amounts of snow, our neighborhood became covered with large, blowing drifts of the white stuff, like white ocean waves all over the ground. Some of the drifts actually covered the cars in the driveways, and a few houses were half-buried in snow. Our little house had snow right up to the windowsills.

During those two weeks your mom and I stayed inside—it was too stormy and cold to go outside. Mother had bought a lot of food before Christmas, but by now it was almost all gone. And we were just about out of firewood. In fact, Mother had just put the last of it in the kitchen woodstove to cook breakfast and heat some bath water. The wood-burning furnace in the basement was almost out of fuel as well. Over some hot porridge, Mother said, "Bobby, I think you're going to have to cut a path through the snow to the woodpile. If we don't get more wood in the house, we're going to freeze." This came as a shock. Dad always got the wood.

You may wonder why this shocked me. Well, even though Dad had been away for two weeks, it wasn't the first time he'd been gone that long. In fact, one of his absences had lasted two months. So in the back of my mind, I fully expected him to come back. But this time was different, Mother had told us. This time he wasn't coming back. I guess I didn't really believe her. I still expected him to return. But hearing that I'd have to shovel all that snow and get the wood jolted me back to reality. Dad was gone for good.

I bundled up in my warmest winter clothes and went out the kitchen door to the back porch. The porch was like a small wooden shed attached to the house. It had two windows, one on each side, and a wooden door. In the winter it was as cold inside as outside. The windows had a thick layer of ice on them, and the door was covered with frost. I picked up the shovel and went out.

Fortunately, the door was between drifts, and I pushed it open fairly easily. But the size of the job ahead made my heart sink. Our lot was very large, and it was about one hundred feet to the pile of firewood. I couldn't see the wood, mind you; it was completely covered with snow (even though the woodpile was five feet tall!). And the path I had to dig was through snow piled anywhere from three feet to six feet deep. I didn't think I could do it. *Dad could, if he were here,* I thought. I bit back the tears and started to dig.

My friend from next door, Darryl Krause, saved the day. About a half-hour after I'd started to dig, he came over on a pair of skis. He surprised me—I had my head down, picking up a heavy shovelful, when I heard his voice high above me. "Hi, Bobby! What ya doin'?" I looked up and there was Darryl, his skis level with my head. He was grinning at me.

"What's it look like I'm doin'?" I replied, delighted to see him.

"How come you're doin' this? Where's your dad?" he asked.

"Oh, he's away," I answered.

"When's he comin' back?" he asked.

"Uhmm, in a few days," I lied. If it hadn't been so cold I would have blushed with the lie. But my face was already as red as it could get.

I explained to him that I was trying to get to the woodpile. "Well, you're never gonna get there that way," he said. "Wait a minute. I've got an idea. Get your sister's sled, and I'll get my brother's skis." In a few minutes Darryl and I were towing icy pieces of wood, piled on your mom's sled, over the snow to our back porch. It was fun—even though it took a while getting used to his brother's skis. Within an hour we had as much wood as we'd need in a week.

That night as I lay in bed I wondered why I had lied to Darryl about Dad. Was it because I was embarrassed? Ashamed? Hurt? Or was it because I was jealous of Darryl and his happy home? I decided I had lied for all those reasons and more. Deep down in my heart I felt abandoned. Trying to do a man's job had shown me how little, weak, and young I really was. I was only ten, after all. And as tough as it had been to live with Dad, he was still my dad, and I missed him. I cried myself to sleep.

The next morning as I lay in the warmth of my bed, I remembered something Mother had said on Christmas Day. "Don't ever forget, children, that the three of us love each other very much. There are some unhappy children who have no one to love them. Remember, there is always something to be thankful for." I decided that morning to be thankful. And you know what? I had a great day!

In the next letter I'm going to tell you the story of my first dog. His name was Rocky.

Give our love to your mom. Aunt Jenny sends her love to you both. I'll write you again on Thursday.

Love you,
Uncle Bob

3

Dear Jess and Kate,

Hi! How are you? Aunt Jenny and I really enjoyed your letters. We especially liked the picture you sent from last winter—the snow was nearly as high in your backyard as it was that winter I talked about in my last letter. Snow can be such fun! Except when you have to shovel it.

In my last letter I promised to tell you about our first pet, a dog named Rocky. Your mom and I named him after the heavyweight boxing champion of the world at that time, Rocky Marciano. Here's how Rocky the dog came into our lives.

Spring had sprung. In fact, we'd just had the first week of warm weather. All that snow had begun to melt, and little rivers were running in the ditches. We didn't have sewers in those days, so every home had a ditch between the front yard and the gravel road. Under each driveway was a large cement pipe (or culvert) that kept the ditch water flowing from one side of the driveway to the other. I used to love making boats out of wood and floating them down those ditches and through the culverts. Your mom and I used to race our boats from our house all the way down to Mayor Davidson's house at the corner. It wasn't speed that won (both boats went at the same speed); the culverts decided the winner. Most of them had all kinds of unseen snags. Often both boats would enter one side of a culvert and only one would come out on the other side. Then the person with the stuck boat (usually me, because I always built a bigger one than your mom) would have to wait and wait, or else try to find a pole and poke at both ends of the culvert. Many times I'd get wet up to my shoulder or even fall in! Then I'd rush home, freezing, and have to spend an hour in front of the woodstove thawing out.

One day Olaf and Molly Sandstrom from across the street were racing boats with us. Both of them had white-blonde hair. Olaf had a brush cut (shaved on the sides, short and bristlelike on the top), and Molly had straight shoulder-length hair with bangs. Olaf was quite chubby and very strong, while Molly was slim and very pretty (at least, I thought so—your mom wasn't so sure). They had moved to Butte two years before from Norway. And they spoke English with a funny accent. Olaf, Molly, and your mom had just reached Mayor Davidson's with their boats (mine was stuck in front of Krauses') when we heard Mrs. Sandstrom's high voice calling, "Ola-a-f! Mol-l-ly!" Since I was closer to their house I repeated the call: "Olaf! Molly! Your mom wants you!" I saw them take their boats out of the ditch and race home. I knew why they were running so fast. Their cocker spaniel, Boots, was very pregnant. Maybe the pups were coming!

7

Sure enough, a few minutes later, Olaf came rushing out of their house calling loudly, "Bobby! Suzy! Come quick! Boots has had her pups!"

"How many?" your mom asked breathlessly as we ran around to their back porch. "Seven," Olaf answered with excitement, "and their eyes are all closed over!" I wasn't sure if that was bad news or good news, but we scrambled onto the porch, threw off our boots and coats, and entered the kitchen to see the blind pups.

There in a towel-lined washtub beside the woodstove lay Boots with her babies. They were wriggling, squeaking, and burrowing into Boots's tummy, while she was calmly and proudly licking their fuzzy little bodies. I looked with alarm at their closed eyes, but Mrs. Sandstrom quickly told us that all pups were born that way and soon their eyes would open. Molly picked one up and gave it to your mom, who promptly began to mother it with cooing sounds and snuggles. I thought it looked a bit ugly with its pink paws, pink lips, short hair, and pudgy face. "Looks like a hairy frog," I said, and got nothing but scornful looks from your mom.

Then, from the bottom of the squirming pile, the ugliest pup of all emerged. He was about half the size of the others and looked half-dead. Olaf picked him up. "This is the runt," he said. "He probably will die."

"Oh, no!" Molly cried, and she quickly snatched it from Olaf.

"Careful!" warned Mrs. Sandstrom. Then Molly began mothering the pitiful pup.

He really *was* pitiful. The others may have looked like hairy frogs, but this one looked like a bald duck. He had a very narrow head and fat, bill-like lips. His legs resembled toothpicks and his feet oversized sneakers. One ear looked like a featherless chicken wing. Even though his eyes were closed, this bent ear made him look curious, as if he were about to ask questions about the meaning of life. I thought to myself, *If this pup makes it, he's gonna be one strange-looking mutt. He's gonna be a character!* I fell in love with him immediately.

So did your mom. For different reasons, mind you. I saw him as the weirdest-looking dog in town, galumphing around with me as I played road hockey or built tree forts with my friends. He'd be one of the gang—a sort of doggy pirate or town thief. Your mom saw him as a poor, sick, afflicted orphan who would die in anyone's care but her own. That's why we both asked at the same time, "Mrs. Sandstrom, can we have the runt?" Her answer? You guessed it—"Only if your mother says you can." Boy! Did we run home fast!

It wasn't easy. Right away Mother said no. Not, "No, dears," but no as in "That's final!" But your mom and I wouldn't take no for an answer. We pled. We wept. We whined. We promised all kinds of things. "If you let us have him, I'll never complain again about going to bed at 7:30 or having a bath every night." (That was me—I couldn't believe I was saying it.) And your mom said, "If you let us have him, Bobby and I will always pick up our toys, clean our rooms, and make our beds every morning." *(That is going a bit far,* I thought. *Why is she including me?)* But then I thought of the runt pirate and cried loudly, "That's right, Mom! Never a messy room ever, ever!" When you want a dog you'll promise anything.

The issue was settled a few days later. The pups' eyes had opened by then, but the runt wasn't doing well. His body weight was low—mainly because he couldn't fight his way through his brothers and sisters to Boots's milk. He was clearly dying. He was thin, his eyes were watery and unfocused, and he shivered a lot. We managed to get Mother over to see him in his pitiful state, and that was it. Mother, like your mom, couldn't resist him. We brought him home, and within minutes he was wrapped in a warm blanket and Mother was heating some milk. Rocky had found a home.

I'll tell you more about Rocky in the next letter. But there's something important to remember about his story so far—it has to do with fairness. It wasn't fair that he was born so small. It wasn't fair that his brothers and sisters outmuscled him for the milk. It wasn't fair that he was ugly. In fact, if Rocky had been able to understand his sorry condition, he might have shaken his "fist" at the world and wept bitterly because nobody seemed to care. But he couldn't, and he didn't. What's more, Rocky had a future. He couldn't see it, but your mom and I could. And what a future that was to be!

Even though your parents have divorced, I want you to know that you've got a future too. A great one! You may not see it, but your mom and I do. How do I know this? For one reason—you're loved. Your mom loves you; Aunt Jenny and I love you. And God loves you too. For Rocky, love made all the difference.

I'll write again next week.

Love ya,
Uncle Bob

4

Dear Jess and Kate,

Uh-oh! Seems I created a little problem with my last letter. Your mom called me a few days ago and told me you've really put on the pressure to get a dog! After your mom's call, Aunt Jenny said, "I told you so! You shouldn't have told them about Rocky." Well, I don't know. What I *do* know is that it's your mom's decision. Maybe now is not the time for a dog. But at the risk of getting your mom even madder at me, I'm going to continue Rocky's story. After all, I promised, didn't I?

Actually, what I want to tell you about Rocky in this letter has a lot to do with what you're dealing with right now. You want a dog. Today! Not tomorrow, or at Christmas, or for your birthday. You want it now. And it's very upsetting to be refused, *especially* when you know that your mom had a dog when she was your age. "It's not fair," I can hear you saying, Jess. Or "How come you can and we can't?" says Kate. Well, the question is not really one of fairness; it's one of patience. Let's get back to Rocky.

The first few days Rocky was with us, we were totally caught up in caring for him. Feeding him was tough—we gave him his warm milk with an eyedropper (if you don't know what that is, I'm sure your mom will show you one). Then, after a couple of days, we finally got him to drink from a baby bottle. Your mom loved it, of course. It was kind of like feeding a real baby doll all wrapped up in a cuddly blanket. But the doll was so ugly! And it left all kinds of smelly, yucky deposits on its blankets—which *I* had to wash! Ugh!

Then there was the question of where Rocky was to sleep. Your mom thought he should sleep with her, but Mother said no. We decided that a small box near the woodstove would be best. "We've got to keep him warm," your mom said. The problem, however, was just that. Keeping him warm meant keeping a fire going at *all* times. Which meant nighttime. Middle-of-the-night time! Guess who got to get up at night and add wood to the fire? You guessed it. Me!

Because of this I thought it would be nice for me to stay home from school for a few days, or at least until Rocky was healthy and strong. "How about if I stay home from school for a month, Mother?" I asked, trying to keep a look of deep concern for Rocky on my face.

"Forget about that, young man," she replied. (She always called me "young man" when I asked for or did something that was usually described as ridiculous.) "That's a totally ridiculous idea," she added. *There she goes again,* I thought.

It seemed to take forever for Rocky to get healthy. In fact, in those first weeks there were moments when we thought he might not make it. One critical moment occurred when I went rushing out to play with Olaf on a cold spring morning and forgot to close the back door. Mother was in the basement washing clothes, and your mom was up in her room—which meant that Rocky was exposed to a cold draft for about an hour. He caught cold and nearly died. The next few days were really tense. Not only did he shiver all the time (even in his blanket), but he coughed with such violence that his little ribs looked like they would break. I felt awful. The looks your mom gave me during these coughing fits didn't help either. Sometimes sisters can be a pain! (Okay, I know, so can brothers.)

The thing that surprised me in all of this caring for Rocky was how quickly caretaking became a chore. Work! There was no fun in it—at least, for me there wasn't. Your mom enjoyed mothering him. But even for her the work got to be a bit much.

You see, I wanted a doggy-friend. And all I was getting, so far, was a royal pain! A doggy-invalid. And as much as I cared for Rocky, life still had to go on. I still wanted to play with my friends. I still wanted to go exploring in the woods. But no. I had to stay close to home, keep the fire going, and care for Rocky. This little mutt was ruining my life. At least, that's how I felt.

Amazing, huh? There I was, just a few days ago, pledging my undying devotion to the feeble runt, promising Mother that there'd never be a speck of dust or a cast-off sock in my room again. Then—I hated to admit it—I was wishing we'd never taken Rocky home. Why do you suppose I felt this way? Was it that I was lazy? That could be part of it. But I think it was more than that; I was impatient. I hated to wait. It was taking too long for Rocky to get well and grow up.

Waiting is never easy. I remember when I planted my first garden. I was five at the time. There was a very large vacant lot beside our house that nobody seemed to own. Things were pretty casual in those days—as it happened, we found out many years later that the lot belonged to us! Anyway, I guess things had been pretty tough that past winter. Dad had been drinking heavily and had spent a lot of our food money on himself. So Mother decided to grow her own food. As soon as the snow melted and the ground softened up, she was out in that lot measuring the boundaries of a garden.

Planting a garden isn't easy. Before you do anything else, you've got to get rid of all the weeds and stuff that grow on the surface. One sunny spring Saturday morning I looked out the bedroom window and saw Mother cutting the weeds and long grass with a scythe. What's a scythe? The simplest description I can think of is a long, curved knife with a handle like this:

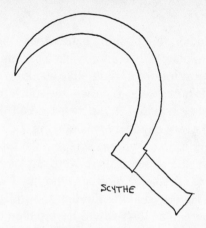

SCYTHE

Sort of like something from a horror movie, isn't it? But, as tough and dirty and scratchy as that job was, there was something even tougher to do.

When she'd finished scything, the lot looked like it had been flattened by a tropical storm. It had a scrubby, uneven, wounded look, like some bearded man who'd had his beard torn out by an angry mob. But now she had to start turning that ugly scrub over with a garden shovel, or spade, as we called it. You can't believe how tough this is. I remember watching her huffing, puffing, and wiping her long hair out of her eyes—back bent, hands dirty, her thin dress stained with sweat. It really was a back-breaking job; every time she jammed the spade into the earth she'd strain to break the hold of the grass roots and turn the clump over. Then she'd have to grab the grass that held the clump together and hit it four or five times on the ground to free the grass from the dirt. Then she would toss whatever was left in her hand onto a pile she intended to burn later. I don't think I've ever seen anyone work harder than she did digging that garden.

She didn't have a garden yet, by the way. She still had to chop away at the clumps to break them down into smaller clumps, and then she had to use a garden rake to break those clumps into nice, even, soft soil. After that she dug the soil into long rows of shallow trenches, in which she would plant the seeds. This is the part where I got involved. She gave me a small corner to plant my own garden. (For some reason, your mom didn't want a corner for herself—maybe because she was only four. Or maybe she figured, after watching Mother, that planting gardens was too much like work!) I decided to plant only carrots. I liked carrots.

But, as I've already told you, I didn't like waiting. And a garden takes time. Carrots take weeks to grow—too much time for me.

Every day I went out to look at the rows where I'd planted the carrot seeds. And every day there was nothing. I couldn't stand it! One day Mother even caught me scraping the topsoil off one of the rows—I wanted to see if there were any carrot tops just beneath the surface. Then, one glorious morning, I went out and there were green shoots breaking through the soil! Fortunately Mother was in the garden, or I would have pulled them all out right then. As it was, she convinced me to let them alone.

Every day the shoots got bigger. Then they started growing leaves. And every morning they were just a bit taller. After about two weeks they were two to three inches tall and very leafy. I just couldn't take it anymore! So I pulled one up. To my amazement the carrot was a scrawny white root, thinner than a drinking straw and only about half an inch long. *This must be a sick one,* I thought. So I pulled up another. And another. And another. "They're all sick," I exclaimed to myself. Just then Mother came out and halted my destruction of the carrots. Several weeks later I *did* pull out juicy, tasty, full-size carrots. But there were a lot less than there might have been, because of my impatience. I hated to wait. But I learned that you've got to wait for carrots!

Like I said, waiting isn't easy. It wasn't easy waiting for Rocky to grow healthy. It wasn't easy waiting for the carrots to develop. And, as you know, it's *never* easy waiting for Christmas morning. Waiting is hard.

And you know what? Waiting is as tough for me now as it was when I was your age. And it's the same for everyone. Nobody likes to wait. But we've all got to do it.

That's why doing what you've got to do during a period of waiting is important. The daily duties of caring for a sick puppy, weeding a young garden, or doing homework (when all you want is to get out of school and into a *long,* very long, summer vacation) not only keep you busy, but also keep you focused on the goal. The goal may be a healthy, happy doggy-friend, crunchy carrots, or delicious summer days at the lake. But what makes your days so sweet when that dog is grown up, or those carrots so tasty, or the summer so wonderful, is what you've had to go through to get to that point. Waiting adds value to life.

Speaking of waiting, I'm waiting eagerly for your next letters. Aunt Jenny and I love to hear from you. And next Thursday I'll be writing you again. I really enjoy my write-Jess-and-Kate-days. I can hardly wait!

Love you,
Uncle Bob

5

Dear Jess and Kate,

Hi! Thanks for your letters. Not only were they very interesting, but the pictures you drew of Rocky were great! Thanks also (to your mom?) for the package of carrot seeds. Very funny. Now Aunt Jenny wants me to plant them in the backyard, which means I've got to dig a garden. Ugh! Work! Who needs it! All thanks to you . . . just kidding!

In my last letter I mentioned how tough it is to wait. And that made me think of waiting for summer vacation. The months of May and June used to be an agony for me. I'd sit in class and spend most of my time staring out the window. I loved summers—especially the ones we spent on Manitoulin Island at Rainbow Village. I remember our first time there. I was nine and your mom was seven. We had a very hot summer that year. Uncle Bill and Aunt Edna were just young adults then and had purchased the resort on Lake Kagawong that past winter. They had worked long and hard during the spring to get ready for the tourists. As soon as school was out, your mom and I moved to the resort and lived there all summer. Mother had a short break and then joined us a month later.

Did your mom ever tell you that before Uncle Bill bought the resort, it was called Bert's Camp? The former owner, whose name really was Bert, lived in one of the cabins that summer until his new house in Spring Bay was built and ready. He was a nice old guy. He treated your mom and me real well—in fact, he taught us how to pick dew worms at night in the rain. I don't think he was too happy when Uncle Bill changed the name to Rainbow Village.

It was Bert who told us how to beat the heat. With only a week to go before the first tourist guests arrived, Uncle Bill and Aunt Edna were finishing some work on the dock. Bert got their permission to take us for a hike. Rainbow Village, as you know, has a huge amount of land with over two miles of shoreline. So we hiked to the northern tip of the property at Jackson's Point.

In those days Jackson's Point was all wooded, and the swamp that's there today was an almost hidden cove. In fact, people who used to anchor their boats off the point sometimes fished there all day without seeing the cove through the trees. Bert took us by a secret path right to the cove itself. He told us pirates used to camp there centuries ago.

We had a great time! Bert told us pirate stories. We fished, we swam—and, most important—we built a fort in the trees before we left that day. It was a great fort, with three rooms and a lookout. We used pine boughs for walls and an old canvas sail for a roof. The floor was about three inches thick with pine needles. Bert didn't know it (or maybe he did), but in helping us find that cove and build that fort, he was giving your mom and me a lifetime memory. And because the fort was shaded and the water in the cove so cool, Bert also gave us a place, that hot summer, to retreat from the scorching sun.

For the rest of the summer, hardly a day went by without our going to the fort. We often used to pack a lunch. Once Uncle Bill came with us, and we slept overnight in the fort! What a night that was. Three times your mom shook me awake, certain she had heard a bear sniffing outside the walls. Once she got so scared she started to cry, so Uncle Bill built a campfire and assured her that bears were afraid of fires and wouldn't come close. That calmed her.

A few days after the sleepover Bert rowed a beat-up old boat to the cove and pulled it up on shore. From then on we not only had a fort; we also had a battleship. We used to dive off it and sit in it and talk. Sometimes we'd turn it over in the water and dive under it, surfacing in the air bubble beneath its capsized bottom, and pretend we were shipwrecked.

I guess the thing that strikes me as most important about these memories is the talks your mom and I used to have. We'd sit in the fort or the boat and talk about everything. One of the big subjects was what we'd be when we grew up. That first year your mom wanted to be a nurse. The next year a teacher. A few years later (when she was twelve) she wanted to be a doctor. Me? I never knew what I wanted to be. But one thing we both agreed on—if ever we married and had kids, we'd always look out for each other.

Well, that's easy to say and hard to do. When your mom and I made that promise to look out for each other, it hadn't occurred to us that in our adult lives we might live so many hundreds of miles apart. Nor did we imagine that one day she would be raising two wonderful kids alone. Well, it's very hard for me to think of her without a husband—and to think of you two without an everyday dad. I know you get to see him occasionally, but I'll bet you wish he'd never left. I know you feel bad about it. So do I.

By the way, it's okay to feel bad. I know that doesn't make you feel better, but don't ever feel guilty about feeling bad. And don't ever feel guilty about feeling good either. Just try always to do what you know is right. When you do what's right, you have a clean conscience. When your conscience is clean you can always control your feelings, whether good or bad—your feelings won't control you.

But getting back to that promise your mom and I made to each other in the fort— it's been very difficult for me to know what to do for her and for you. My first thought was to invite you to come and live with us. But that wouldn't work. For one thing, it would mean taking you from your home and friends and school, and that would be too much for you. It's a big enough adjustment just getting used to your dad being gone. Plus, our house isn't big enough anyway. My second thought was for Aunt Jenny and I to move closer to you. But that won't work either—my company doesn't have a branch in your town. And I'm not sure it would help much anyway. The last thing your mom needs is her older brother living close, where he can give her free advice every day. I tend to say too much too often.

I'm not sure I've learned fully that there's a big difference between *caring* and *interfering*. Caring means you are concerned enough to make yourself available to help and to give your opinion when asked. Interfering means you force yourself and your opinion on the person you're concerned about. Caring is always helpful. Interfering is seldom helpful. Interfering means I force my help on you *now*. Caring means I wait for the best time and circumstance. Caring takes patience (which is one of my weak points—remember my last letter and the carrots?).

But you know what I *am* learning? I'm learning that one of the best things I can do for your mom is to be a good listener. Just being available by phone to listen to her express her needs is a step toward meeting those needs.

Have you ever noticed that after talking with a good friend about your troubles, those troubles have less weight? The problem with interfering types, like me, is that we want to carry more of the load than we can or should. The best care is often shown by just listening to the one you care about. When you listen, you share the load, and you help your friend bear the load at the same time.

Well, enough wisdom for now! I just want to encourage you to do for each other what your mom and I are learning to do—share your thoughts together and be good listeners.

Someone who loves you and listens to you is a great treasure.

Lots of love,
Uncle Bob

6 _____ ✍

Dear Jess and Kate,

Thanks for your letters. Your picture of the bear, Kate, was fr-r-rightening! And Jess, the picture of your mom and me playing in the boat was super! Was that a pirate's face in one corner? Scar-r-ry! You both are good artists!

Speaking of scary, I remember a night when your mom scared me so much I thought I would die. Now, when I think of it, it's quite a funny story. But it wasn't so funny then. Here's what happened.

The Christmas after Dad left, we spent the holiday at Uncle Bill and Aunt Edna's place in Providence Bay. Their home was about thirty miles from Rainbow Village. The winds swept off Lake Huron and swooped up and over the snow-covered sand dunes. Those snowy dunes made great toboggan hills. We'd race down them so fast that sometimes we slid all the way to the chunks of ice at the shore. Then we'd climb all the way up and rush down again. After a few hours of this—and it was exhausting!—we'd make one final climb, walk about a hundred yards to the other side of the dunes where we could see the town, and then slide down almost to Uncle Bill and Aunt Edna's house. What fun!

Aunt Edna would always have a mug of hot chocolate ready, and your mom and I would take off our snowy clothes and boots and sit by the woodstove with our thawing feet propped in front of the oven! No kidding! I'll never forget the feeling of my ice-cold feet starting to thaw out. It hurt! But it was a pleasant kind of hurt.

I remember that sometimes we'd be having such fun that our final slide for the day took place as darkness was descending on Providence Bay. I used to love looking down from the dunes at the lights of the town—especially the lights of Uncle Bill and Aunt Edna's little home. I remember your mom once saying to me, "Look at their house, Bobby, look at how cuddly it is!" And it was. It was a cuddly, homey house that sort of reached out its arms to us.

These were the days before television came to Providence Bay. Television existed, but not for this town. Providence Bay was too far from the television station in the big city. I know how hard it must be for you to imagine a world without TV. But it wasn't so bad.

One of the things the people in the neighborhood did for entertainment in those long winter evenings was to get together at someone's home for sharing supper and storytelling. On one of those nights, when about thirty neighbors came to Uncle Bill and Aunt Edna's house, your mom scared me half to death.

As people came to the door that night, Uncle Bill took their heavy winter coats, scarves, and hats, and piled them on top of the bed in the guest bedroom. By the time everyone had arrived, there was a huge mound of coats and stuff on the bed. Your mom and I loved it! We jumped onto that heap and burrowed into it. It was especially fun in the dark because I'd find my way through the mound with my face. Sometimes my face would be up against a soft wool scarf; then it would brush a scratchy, smelly, wet wool coat. But my favorites were the fur coats that would suddenly reach out to stroke my face. This activity was like swimming blindfolded through a sea of touch-and-smell. I say smell, not just because those wet wool coats smelled wet, but because many of the women's coats had the fragrance of that night's perfume. We had fun guessing which coat belonged to whom.

Well, this particular night there were six or seven other children burrowing with us through the coat hill. After a few minutes we were tunneling not only through the coats, but between the mattress and the box spring, and even under the bed—sometimes wrapped in two or three coats at a time. Then we started telling ghost stories in the dark. One boy was telling the most scary story about a bear-shaped ghost that used to live under the bed of old Granny Jones on Main Street. The ghost used to suddenly jump out at her from under her bed, and she'd "take a fit," as her granddaughter Ardith used to say. Each time he had the ghost jumping out, he'd spread his hands like claws and roar at us. We let out more screams and yells than you can imagine.

Just as he was about to jump at us one more time, suddenly a black, fur-covered shape leaped at us from beneath the bed with a blood-curdling growl! It was so sudden and so real that we all screamed. Becky Anderson started to cry, and Billy Organ later admitted he "wet himself." As for me, I leaped back from this black monster and cracked my head on the bedpost. My heart was beating so furiously it nearly broke out of my chest. Then we heard a giggle from within the black fur. It was your mom, in Becky Anderson's mom's coat.

Later that night, after everyone had gone, your mom and I tried to go to sleep. We couldn't. All I could see was this furry monster jumping at me. And even your mom was scared. True, she had been the monster, but she'd gotten into her role so much that somehow monsters had become more real to her than they'd ever been. She insisted that we sleep with the light on. Even then we checked at least a dozen times under the bed. But all we ever saw were dust balls.

Have you ever been afraid of the dark? Or wondered if there were monsters under your bed? If you have, you're not alone. I think everyone knows what fear is. Especially fear of what you can't see.

This is what is most scary about death. Jess, your mom told me on the phone about your teacher's mother, who died last week. When someone whom we know dies, we're suddenly aware of and afraid of what death really is. Is it the end of everything? Or do we somehow live on in another world? Is there a heaven? If so, what's it like?

The fearful thing about all these questions is that we don't know for sure what the answers are. We can turn to the Bible and read there about heaven, but sometimes it's hard to take somebody real, like your teacher's mother, and relate her to something that is described in a book.

I think the thing to do is to trust your heart. Does your heart tell you that there is a God and that He has a home called heaven? Does it seem true to you somehow that there is more to life than what we see here on earth? Can you believe that when people you love die and go to heaven, they are happy there and are looking forward to your joining them someday? If you can, then you can also be happy in your heart because you believe that life never really ends. We'll all be together again someday forever. This makes me very happy.

I can hardly wait for your next letters. Will it include a picture of a huge, black, ugly, scary bear again?

Aunt Jenny and I love you.
Uncle Bob

7

Dear Jess and Kate,

Whew! Was I ever glad to hear there are no monsters under your bed, Kate! You checked ten times, huh? And pardon me, Jess, for even suggesting you were afraid of ghosts. I forgot that "only little kids have that problem." It was nice of you, though, to agree to have your mom put a night-light in your room, "just in case Kate needs help in the night." You're a good brother! And I'm sure you both miss your dad being there at night.

Have you ever noticed that when you don't want to sleep, your mom says you have to; and when there's nobody telling you to sleep, you do? For example, you're all driving in the car on a trip somewhere. There's all kinds of interesting stuff to see out the window, and the next thing you know your mom's waking you up and telling you the trip's over. Or you're watching a good movie on TV, feeling warm and cozy, and suddenly you're being tucked into bed. "How did I get here?" you may find yourself asking. "You fell asleep watching TV," your mom answers. "Have a good sleep!"

Then there are the times when your mom says, "Time for bed," and going there is the last thing you want to do. You complain, but she says, "No. It's your bedtime. Off you go! Don't forget to brush your teeth!" And you go to your room, put on your pajamas, go to the bathroom, and brush your teeth—complaining all the while. You hear your mom's voice in the kitchen loudly telling you how good sleep is for you. It makes you a better student; it keeps you from being grouchy . . . and you feel about as grouchy at this moment as you have all day! Sleep. Who needs it?!

Did your mom ever tell you about the time our grandfather had to fight off sleep in a blizzard? If she did, forgive me for telling you the story again; but you probably haven't heard it.

Mother's parents were living about fifteen miles from Billings, Montana, and Mother was only three months old. Their little farm was out in the middle of nowhere, but Gramps and Gran were able to make a living. That winter, Mother's first on earth, was one of the worst in Montana's history.

A huge snowstorm had been raging for three weeks. The wind blew solidly from the east for twenty-one days, something the old-timers in the state had never seen happen before. The snow drifted, creating huge banks that covered everything, including houses and some telephone poles. And because the wind had most of flat Montana to build up speed, it was a full-blown blizzard by the time it reached Billings.

Gran and Gramps had been unable to get supplies during those days. In fact, Gramps had to shovel his way out of the house each day just to care for the animals in the barn. In your family album, there may be a picture of the farm that Gramps took a day or so after the storm ended. Ask your mom if she can find it. What a sight!

By week two of the blizzard, Gran was out of milk. Mother was their first baby, and in those days many new mothers thought it was better to feed a baby from a bottle rather than with mother's natural milk. So Gran fed Mother evaporated milk—that was all she had.

This was an emergency, of course. What were they to do? Mother wasn't aware of the storm and had a constant need for food. The car was totally covered in snow, and so were the country roads. So Gramps decided the only thing he could do was to walk to Billings.

Gran was torn between her fear of her baby starving and of Gramps freezing, but there really was no choice. Telling Gran he might not be back until the next day, Gramps set out.

He told me that it wasn't too hard at first. He had two things in his favor. The first was that the snow had been drifting with such power that it was hard-packed; the snow would hold his weight. Second, the road to Billings was straight, and Gramps could see its outline even though he was walking ten feet above it on the snowpack. The telephone lines were almost like handrails marking his path. Occasionally he would break through the snow with one foot, and sometimes with both feet, and then find himself up to his waist. But he managed to keep going. And he made it to the general store in about eight hours.

I guess he was quite a sight when he got there. The store was open, sort of. The owner, Mr. Carter, had dug a path down to his front door, and several hardy customers were keeping him pretty busy. But when Gramps got there, everyone stared at him in amazement. They told him that he looked like a snowman. His whole body was white. And he was huffing and puffing like one of those old steam engines you've seen in the TV movies. But he made it.

That night he slept on Mr. Carter's floor and left the next morning at about seven. The storm had been blowing very hard overnight, and Gramps had a more difficult time seeing the telephone wires. It was also colder, mainly because on his way home Gramps had to walk into the wind. What's more, he had a thirty-pound box of canned milk on his shoulder, made even heavier and bulkier by the blanket he had wrapped it in to keep the milk from freezing.

On top of all this, Gramps had exhausted himself the day before. That's why the walk back was, in his own words, "the toughest thing I've ever done in my life."

About halfway back he thought he might not make it. The added weight had caused him to break through the snowpack "at least a hundred times," and he just had no energy left. His body was numb, and his mind was starting to play tricks on him. For instance, at one point Gramps actually started to take his coat off because he felt too warm. Then he remembered that your mind gets all confused when you're freezing, so he kept it on. At another point he thought he saw a well-lit service station and smelled hamburgers cooking. But it was just a mirage.

He thought he'd just lie down and rest a while. As he lay there he started feeling warm and sleepy. He dozed off for a minute, then awoke with a start. His body felt a sudden charge of fear as he remembered that this warmth and sleep were a sure sign he was freezing to death. So he threw snow on his face, got up, and continued walking. "The thought of Gran alone and the baby starving kept me going," he later told me. That was not a time for sleep.

Gran always said the sight of Gramps stumbling in the door that night was the most wonderful thing she'd ever seen. Within minutes Mother was chomping away on a long-awaited bottle, and Gramps fell asleep with his clothes on in front of the woodstove.

"Remember, Bobby," Gramps said to me when I was about ten years old, "there's a time to sleep and a time not to sleep." Believe me, I've never forgotten that lesson.

There'll come a day when your mom won't be sending you off to bed. You'll send yourself. Why? Because you can usually trust your body when it tells you it's tired. But don't forget that sometimes your mind will have to tell your body to sleep later. There are things more important than sleep. Just as it happened with Gramps, sometimes it takes determination to get that important thing done.

Looking forward to your letters,
Uncle Bob

8 ✍

Dear Jess and Kate,

I've just been reading the paper. There's a neat story there about a woman in Florida who just gave birth to *six* babies! Six! Can you believe it? What makes this story really amazing is that all six are alive. Usually in a birth of this sort, one or two of the babies are born dead or die a few hours later. But not this group! All six are alive and well.

Mind you, they're in *incubators* (check that word in your dictionary), but the doctors expect them to do well. Oh! I almost forgot—they all weigh less than two pounds each! Amazing, huh? What's even more amazing is how a baby is made. Let me tell you about it.

I'm sure you noticed long ago that boys and girls are different from one another, not just below the waist, but also in their interests. But it's that "below the waist" stuff that I'd like to discuss for a few minutes.

As you know, boys have penises and girls have vaginas. You might say that boys have external, and girls have internal "plumbing."

Kate may be surprised to know, Jess, that sometimes your penis doesn't just hang there. Sometimes it sticks up. When this happens it's called an erection, and it can happen quite often. An erection is what will allow you, when you're grown up, to enter your wife's vagina and release the sperm necessary to make a baby. Sperm are little microscopic seeds that will one day be manufactured by those two little testicles hanging in that sac beneath your penis.

Jess may be surprised to know, Kate, that even though your "plumbing" is inside, you already have thousands of microscopic eggs stored up in your tummy. When you're a few years older, these will be released once a month into your uterus. The uterus is better known as the womb. It's a very small area inside your lower tummy that has the remarkable ability to stretch and stretch to hold a developing baby when you and your husband succeed in making one someday. The eggs are stored in two little capsules called *ovaries*. A girl's ovaries and a boy's testicles are about the same size. A baby is the result of one of those eggs being penetrated by a single sperm. When this happens, the egg divides over and over and attaches itself to the lining of the womb, where it grows until nine months later a fully developed baby is born! It's really amazing! (And, as your mom will tell you, it's really hard work—birth, that is. But it's worth it—it produced you two! Right?)

But there's a big question that I'll bet both of you are thinking about. Why? Why would a man ever want to put his penis inside his wife's vagina? And why would she want it to happen? What's going on here? (By the way, adults call this action *making love*.)

It's sort of like hunger. You know what it's like to leave the breakfast table all full of warm oatmeal and toast. You're so full you couldn't eat another thing. But a strange thing happens as you're sitting in class and playing at recess. Your stomach starts letting you know that it's getting empty. *Pain* is too strong a word, but there is a sort of dull ache that begins to grow. It gets stronger and stronger, so much so that before lunch you can hardly wait for the bell to ring. When you eat your lunch, the ache goes away. But by the time suppertime rolls around, you're fighting that ache all over again.

Well, as you get older you'll discover a hunger for a deep, personal friendship with someone of the opposite sex. The ache won't be in your stomach; it'll be in your heart. When you finally meet that special someone and fall in love, you'll discover that sometimes the ache will also be in your most private parts. You'll want to be super close to that person; you'll want to touch and be touched by him or her. Your private parts will swell with a hunger for the deepest physical contact that a man and woman can know. You'll kiss, you'll hug, and, as the most natural thing in the world, both of you will want to have what is called *intercourse*. That's right. As strange as it may seem to you now, there will come a day when the thing you'll want to do more than anything else is to make love. That special person will be the only one who can satisfy your hunger. It's really wonderful. It really is.

But there's something you should know. As powerful as making love is, there's something even more powerful. It's called *selfishness*. Selfishness means that you focus on yourself and use other people to please yourself. A lot of people do this with sex. They use other people as objects to satisfy their sexual hunger. It's almost as if other people are dishes listed on a restaurant menu, rather than persons of great value. So they have intercourse with a variety of people, and you know what? Their sexual need may be satisfied for the moment, but their heart need only gets bigger. Believe me when I say that the sexual hunger we all feel as adults is only truly satisfied by a heart-to-heart commitment of love to one person for life. That's why I believe in marriage. I agree with the Bible, which teaches that sex outside of marriage will never satisfy. In fact, it can end up destroying love.

Now, I know that sometimes (too many times!) marriages end. Like your mom and dad's. Unfortunately, selfishness often has something to do with the breakup. One or the other starts looking at someone else as someone they'd like to have sex with, then begins to focus on that person rather than on the marriage partner. Before you know it the two of them are meeting secretly, and intercourse happens. This is what is called *unfaithfulness,* which is just a big word for cheating—cheating on the person you're married to. It's sex all right, but it destroys love.

You see, there's something about love that demands a special bond and trust between two people forever. When that "foreverness" is betrayed, it dies.

I'm not saying, by the way, that this is what caused your mom and dad to break up. You'll have to wait until your mom tells you the reason someday. But what I *do* want you to know is that you have the potential to be a lifelong friend of someone special in the future. Why not decide right now that you'll be a faithful husband, Jess, or wife, Kate, for all of your marriage? No cheating.

I remember that when I was a teenager, occasionally I'd see an old couple in their seventies or eighties walking hand in hand, obviously loving each other. I used to think, *Why are they holding hands? Romance and sex are only for young people!* Boy, was I wrong! A couple who commit themselves in marriage to each other forever are setting out on a wonderful adventure of love, sex, companionship, and fun. While you're young, think about and plan for a lifelong relationship. It *can* happen. Aunt Jenny and I know.

Love to you,
Uncle Bob

9

Dear Jess and Kate,

I guess there was something about my last letter that got you, Jess, thinking about what love means. You said about your dad, "I really do love him, but sometimes I don't think I like him." I know exactly how you feel. Let me tell you a story.

It was the summer of 1954, and I was seven years old. Your mom was five. That year we first attended a summer camp operated by a group of churches in Montana. It was called Living Waters but was located on a lake that seemed to be anything but living. It was called Lake Manitou, and ugh, it was the worst lake I'd ever seen.

To get a picture of the lake you've got to imagine its setting. I'll try to describe it to you. Jess, you've got that target for your bow and arrows, right? (Maybe I should say "bow and arrow," because the last time I saw you, you'd lost or broken all the arrows but one!) Well, that target is made up of colored circles that start big on the outer border and get smaller until the last one is just a small circle around a dot in the middle. That's the bull's-eye.

What I want you to imagine is that target with an outer circle that is thirty miles across! Each of the smaller circles is five miles from the former one, and the bull's-eye is an area about the size of a village.

Now I want you to imagine laying that huge target on the ground. Each of those circles is made up of rolling, grass-covered hills that descend to the lowest point in that area—the bull's-eye—Living Waters Camp. Just to help you picture it, here's a rough drawing.

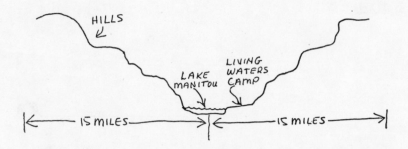

Notice that the camp is on the side of the lowest hill. From there, look down to the middle of the bull's-eye, where Lake Manitou sits.

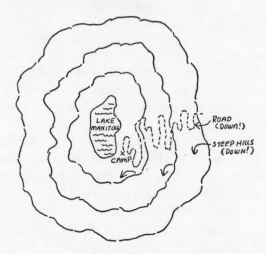

It almost looks like a crater from an ancient meteor strike. Little wonder the hills are called badlands. The terrain looks and feels like something out of an old Western movie. To this day you expect to see cowboys around every curve of that old trail descending the hills.

Now, I've got a question for you. What kind of water do you suppose is in that lake? Notice that any rain would drain down those hills and empty into the lake. But where would the water go after that? Nowhere. Except by evaporation, back into the sky. And what happens when water evaporates?

It leaves behind all the minerals it gathered. Which means? That's right! It means that the lake water becomes full of minerals and salt! Just like the Dead Sea in Israel. Lake Manitou had the foulest, saltiest, unloveliest water I'd ever seen or smelled. It was awful.

So why is Living Waters Camp one of my very favorite boyhood memories? Here's why. For one thing, I remember it fondly because Dad is a part of the memory. He hadn't left us yet, and his drinking problem wasn't as big then as it became later. In fact, our attending Living Waters was his idea. The pastor of a local church, who often visited our home, invited us to attend the camp, but we couldn't afford it. Dad, however, asked, "Reverend Anderson, don't you need some men to help get the camp ready each summer?" To which the pastor responded, "Of course we do." And in a matter of moments it was agreed that we would all go to Living Waters two weeks before it opened—Dad to assist in the preparation and Mother to cook for the work team. Your mom and I went along just for fun.

And what fun it was!

The fun started with the drive to the camp. It was two or three hundred miles to the northeast, which took us right into the flatlands, or prairies, of Montana. The road was gravel, not pavement, which made the trip totally dusty—especially because Dad's old 1936 Chevy was anything but airtight.

I remember the fine dust that filled the air *inside* the car as we bounced along! Mother was wearing a white blouse when we left. By the time we made our first stop for gasoline, her blouse had become gray with dust. In fact, everything inside the car (including us!) was covered with a layer of the stuff. I remember drawing pictures in the dust on the ledge behind the backseat. If your mom and I jumped up and down on the seat, we made a cloud so thick it almost seemed like fog. But, rather than being damp and cold like real fog, this cloud was dry and hot. And adding to the fog were the huge dust trails that billowed up from the cars and trucks in front of us. Sometimes they were so thick that Dad would have to slow down or even stop for a while to be able to see the road. The dust clung to our clothes, stung our eyes, and dried our throats.

Boy! Did we ever enjoy those five-cent Cokes we used to buy at the gas stations. We used to hold the ice-cold green glass bottles to our cheeks before drinking the fizzy soda—it cooled and refreshed us.

After endless miles of dust, we finally came to the edge of the crater I described to you. I'll never forget stopping at that point, getting out of the dusty car, and looking down over the folding hills to Lake Manitou, about fifteen miles below us, gleaming in the late afternoon sun. It was an amazing sight! The grass was so sunburned that the hills looked more like rounded dunes of sand, sort of like pictures I'd seen of deserts in Africa. It looked like another world. And it smelled like one too. I don't know if it was the burned grass, or the tough little flowers that grew there in spite of the heat, or the sulphur gases that sometimes made distant Lake Manitou the smelliest place on earth. Whatever it was, it wasn't unpleasant; the air made us feel more alive in a strange sort of way.

Then we got back into the car and traveled the fifteen miles downhill to Lake Manitou. There were several uphill miles too. Why? Because the crater was lined with descending ridges of hills (remember the picture I drew?), where the tops of ridge two were below the tops of ridge one, and ridge eight was below ridge seven, and so on. But when you drove to the bottom of one ridge you had to climb to the top of the next ridge. In fact, although the trip from the edge of the crater to the lake was only fifteen miles (if you flew down), it was more like forty miles (when you drove down). That's why the trip took at least two hours.

That's right. Two hours! The road was more of a cart path than a proper road. It was full of bumps, huge stones, and treacherous curves. The brakes on Dad's car could hardly handle the strain. That's why he had to stop every mile to let the brakes cool down (hot brakes don't work well). And he often had to put more water in the radiator (from some water bottles he carried in the trunk).

Well, about halfway down I started feeling sick. My stomach started growling and my head started pounding. I knew I was going to throw up. Dad stopped the car, and I hardly made it out the door before being sick. It was terrible!

Things only got worse as we got closer to the camp. The farther down we traveled, the hotter it got. By the time we reached the last ridge before Living Waters, the temperature was at least one hundred degrees. It was so hot that we could smell the grass burning and almost hear it crackling as it turned brown and shriveled in the sun. Even the grasshoppers seemed to be making a strained sound as if complaining about the heat.

The final mile was a very steep slope cutting down the side of the hill directly above the camp. It was especially dusty and bumpy and seemed never to end.

I was caught between the excitement of seeing the buildings and the lake and the agony roaring in my stomach and head. I was thrilled to be there, yet never felt sicker in my life. You might say that at that moment I both loved and hated Living Waters. I loved it; I really did. But I didn't like it. Not at that moment, anyway.

There's so much more to tell you. Wait until you hear about the room we stayed in! And the secret passageways in the main building! And Mickey the bulldog! And the stoneboat! (Don't know what a stoneboat is? Just you wait!) But all of that and more is for future letters.

Aunt Jenny is calling me to lunch. So let me quickly conclude. The point I'm trying to make in this letter is that loving someone or something isn't always easy. Many, many times, when you love someone (like your dad) or a place (like Living Waters), there are things about them that are very unlikable. Sometimes you find something so unlikable you cry out in anger, "I *hate* him," or "I *hate* it." But then you remember the good times and feel confused. I'm sure, Jess and Kate, there are a lot of great memories you have of your dad—just as there are some not-so-great memories and feelings. I want you to know that this is completely normal. Everybody who loves someone or something has feelings similar to yours.

I'll say much more about love in future letters. And there's lots more to tell about Living Waters too. I can't wait!

Aunt Jenny and I love you,
Uncle Bob

10

Dear Jess and Kate,

It's been a while since I told you about Rocky, hasn't it? Last time he was still pretty sick and feeble, and I was getting impatient. I didn't want an invalid; I wanted a healthy, playful doggy-buddy. He *did* become healthy, but then he was nearly killed. Not by accident either, but by Adam Gibson. Here's what happened.

Just about the time I was planting those carrots, Rocky started showing signs of recovery. He began to sit up in his box and put his front paws up on the edge. His eyes began to sparkle, and he even gave an occasional yip when he wanted to be picked up.

One morning when we were eating breakfast, your mom cried, "Oh! Look at Rocky!" We looked, and there he was, his paws on the box's edge, straining to get out. His little head was out of the box, and he was all set to jump. Your mom immediately got out of her chair to go over and pick him up. But Mother said, "No, dear, see if he can do it himself." Almost as if he had heard Mother's challenge, Rocky wriggled further until his body was draped over the edge. Suddenly, with a thud he toppled onto the floor, right on his head! He uttered a frightened yip, then picked himself up. With one floppy ear folded over his head, he looked at us with a face that said, "Look out, world, here I come!" He was almost grinning.

Over the next few days he became so frisky that he was almost a nuisance. He waddled everywhere—under the table, into cupboards, and through all the rooms on the main floor, knocking over anything he could. His exploring was limited to the main floor because he couldn't climb stairs. Nor could he go downstairs. He learned this lesson one day when Mother left the door to the basement open. She was down there washing clothes. Rocky heard the old washing machine grinding away and went to investigate. He walked back and forth at the top step, whining and edging one paw, then the other, over the edge. Suddenly he reached too far and *thump! thump! thump!* He fell all the way to the bottom. Mother rushed over and picked him up. He looked more frightened than hurt. But it was several days before he'd even approach those stairs again!

Soon, of course, he got bored with the house and wanted to go outside. We had been waiting for a hot spring morning (there had been a lot of rain) to let him do just that. We not only wanted to give him his freedom; we also wanted to begin training him to "do his business" outside rather than inside (ugh! *that's* another story!). When the day arrived, it just happened to be a Saturday.

Don't you just love Saturday mornings? Maybe you love them for different reasons than I did. You have all those cartoons on TV, and I know they're fun to watch (I even watch them once in a while!). But in those days we didn't have TV. I used to love to lie in bed, making a tent with the covers draped over my knees and head. The light streaming from the window would filter through the blanket and give a warm, rosy light to the inside of my tent. I used to lie there for hours, sometimes reading a book (like *Tom Sawyer* or *The Yearling*) and sometimes just daydreaming. It was great!

This particular Saturday, however, I jumped out of bed as soon as I saw that it was a sunny morning. I wanted to take Rocky outside immediately. Your mom was still asleep. So was Mother.

I quickly got dressed and went down to the kitchen to get Rocky, but he wasn't in his box.

I found him on the porch sniffing at the door. He seemed to know that today was the day. When he saw me he began to wiggle his back end and yip with excitement. As I put on my shoes he actually started jumping. Well, maybe *jumping* isn't the right word; it was more like hopping on his back legs with his front paws up on the door. I was so excited that I didn't even tie the laces. I opened the door, and Rocky tumbled out.

Unfortunately, there was a small puddle at the bottom of the porch steps. After tripping and thumping down those steps, Rocky fell right into the puddle. But he quickly picked himself up, shook his body to get rid of the water (the first time I'd seen him do that), took a few steps, and then stopped. He raised his nose in the air and stood there for about thirty seconds, sniffing. His little nostrils were moving in and out like a rabbit's. It was as if the outside world had a smell to be identified and registered in the computer of his brain. Then, with that smell in his memory bank, he set out to sniff at everything in his unfolding universe.

Sniff, snuffle, and sneeze. This was the pattern for the first hour. Rocky stuck his nose into everything—tufts of grass, the woodpile, every row of vegetables planted in Mother's new garden. He spent a great deal of time sniffing around the out-house—in fact, he did four complete circuits. He had a few rough moments snuffling into an old rag that Mother had soaked in turpentine to clean a gardening tool. His eyes got all red and watery, and he must have sneezed for five minutes. Once he sneezed so hard that he lost his balance and lurched into a rake leaning against the woodpile. The rake fell down, just slightly grazing his shoulder. He yelped like he'd been shot and tried to run away with such force that he tripped, skidding face first into a pile of garbage that had fallen from an overturned trash can. To my amazement, he seemed to like this stuff. In fact, horror of horrors, he started to *eat* it! I quickly picked him up and, uttering my disgust, took him inside for a cleanup. I felt like washing his mouth with soap!

By the time I had him cleaned up, your mom was awake. Of course, we had to take Rocky out again. We were having great fun with him when Adam Gibson walked by. As soon as I saw him I felt a knot in my stomach. Adam scared me.

Adam lived on the edge of town with two aunts in an old wooden house that looked like it hadn't ever been painted. His aunts were really weird; many of my schoolfriends said they were witches. I'm sure they weren't, but they certainly looked like it. They were identical twins, about sixty years old, and they always wore high-collared, long-sleeved, black dresses and pointed black shoes. They treated Adam like an animal. He slept in a shed at the back of their property on a smelly old mattress on the floor. He didn't even eat with them—they used to leave scraps of food for him outside his shed (they wouldn't go inside), and I don't think he ever had a bath. He didn't go to school, which was just fine with the school authorities. Everybody in town avoided him.

I had always been fascinated by Adam—not just because he was about my age and appeared so much older, but because he seemed so wild and so free. Many times when I was in school or in church I would look out the window and see him walking alone, seemingly without a care in the world. I used to envy his freedom from homework and imagine what it would be like to be on holiday every day of the year. He lived without rules and never had to answer to anyone. He was his own man.

It never occurred to me that he envied me. I took for granted having a house, a sister, a mom, hot meals, schoolmates, and clothes. I didn't know that he used to walk around town late at night and long for a warm, well-lit room where people talked to and loved one another. I didn't know that the one thing he wanted more than anything else in the world was a Christmas tree at Christmas and brightly colored presents with toys inside. I hadn't thought he wanted to read and write. I thought he was happy. I didn't know he was angry.

"Hey kid," he snarled at me, "where'd you get the ugly dog?" Before I could answer, your mom piped up, "He is *not* ugly! He's cute."

"No way!" returned Adam. "I think he's ugly."

Your mom started to cry. I was about to take her and Rocky inside when Rocky went scampering over to Adam and put his front paws up on Adam's ragged pants leg, wiggling his back end and yipping to be picked up. Adam just shook his leg and sent Rocky flying into the ditch. "Keep your mutt away from me, you little jerk," he yelled as he started to walk away.

Well, Rocky was not about to be discouraged so easily. He splashed out of the ditch and ran after Adam, thinking this was great fun. "Rocky," your mom cried, and started to run after him. But Adam had started to run too. I saw him look back at Rocky with an expression that could be described as hateful. He knew Rocky was following him.

Suddenly, with quick and horrible intent, he ran across the road just as Paul Miller was driving past in his gray 1939 Dodge. Rocky, of course, followed Adam and ran right under the car. There was a horrifying little thud! and Rocky was hurled end-over-end into the ditch. Your mom screamed and was nearly hit by the next car as she ran to pick him up. Adam ran away laughing, and I walked over to your mom and Rocky. I was sure he was dead; that's why I walked instead of ran. I didn't want to see what I was about to see. I felt like my heart was going to pound right out of my chest.

We were both relieved to see that he was still breathing, but concerned because of the way he was breathing. It was a quick, wheezing pant that really scared us. There was no blood, but he looked badly hurt, especially his left rear leg, which was already about twice the size of the other one. We rushed him home, calling loudly for Mother.

Mother knew exactly what to do. She gently wrapped Rocky in a warm blanket and held him over her shoulder like a baby. I ran around behind Mother and looked up at Rocky's face. His eyes, which had been sort of glazed a few minutes ago, were clearing up. He was shivering a lot and started to whimper. I knew he was going to be okay when he nuzzled Mother's neck and licked her ear. That's when I started to cry.

"I'm gonna *kill* that Adam," I shouted through my tears. "He did it on purpose! I *know* he did!" My sorrow had turned to anger.

Adam didn't deserve to live. I stormed out of the house looking for a club, a knife, or a rock. I didn't care what weapon I used, as long as I could kill Adam. Mother came running out of the house and stopped me. Putting her arms around me, she said, "I know how you feel, Bobby, but hurting Adam won't help. What's done is done. And Adam is such a sad little boy."

Sad? I hadn't ever thought of Adam as sad. He was happy. Tough. Manly. And an enemy. He had deliberately tried to murder my dog. I hated him.

"Come back in," she said gently. "Rocky needs you." That night I slept on the kitchen floor next to Rocky's box. I didn't sleep very well. Rocky was whimpering; the floor was cold and hard; and my mind was filled with evil thoughts about how I was going to get even with Adam. I imagined pushing him in front of a car or setting his shed on fire. I got a great deal of satisfaction picturing him in jail about to be hanged. I thought maybe poison would be a good way to end his life.

The next day was Sunday, which meant Sunday school. And wouldn't you know it? Our teacher talked to us about loving our enemies!

"Don't ever confuse *love* with *like,* children," she said sweetly. "*Like* is how you feel; *love* is how you act. Even if you feel that you hate someone, you can do what's best for that person. That's what love means: to do what's best for the other person." Then she added, "Why not try to do something good for someone you don't like—you'll see what I mean." I was in no mood for this stuff. I shut my mind and stared out the window.

But you know what? She was right. I'll tell you more about Adam and what I learned about love in another letter. I'll also tell you more about Rocky. Yes, he survived. What a great friend he became!

I'll write again next week.

Love,
Uncle Bob

11 ✍

Dear Jess and Kate,

I'm sitting here at my desk, the fire is blazing in the fireplace, and I'm listening to a Mozart CD as I write to you. Earlier today I was talking to an old schoolchum who called and invited me to lunch. I hadn't seen him for thirty years. (Boy! Do I sound old or what?) It was a very, very interesting talk. Let me tell you his story. His name is Gordon Webster. I call him Gordie.

Gordie was born when his mother was only fifteen years old. She was in her first year of high school and, of course, was unmarried. She had become drunk at a party and, in that mindless condition, had allowed one of the boys to have sex with her. It was the first time she'd ever had sex. Because she was so drunk, she remembered very little of the experience. Imagine her shock when the doctor told her a few weeks later that she was pregnant.

Back in those days it was a great embarrassment to have a child outside of marriage. It was quite common for a pregnant girl's parents to take her out of school and send her away (to a relative's home) until the baby was born. They would explain her absence somehow: "Nancy has gone to her grandparents' home for a few months—she wants to study in a different school for a while" or "The doctor said Nancy needed a warmer climate to help her health condition. She's gone south for a few months." Or they'd make up some other excuse. But the poor girl had very little say in the matter. She would just disappear until the baby was born.

When the time for delivery finally arrived, the baby was immediately placed in a foster home to be cared for until adoption could be arranged. A few days later the teenage mother would return home, and everything would get back to "normal." She would never see her baby again.

This is what happened to Gordie—except that no one was found to adopt him. For five years Gordie was shifted from one foster home to another. Foster homes, just in case you've never heard of them before, are homes where a family takes in children from the social services. They are given money to do this—and, unfortunately, there are *some* people who become foster parents only for the money. Notice, I said "some." There *are* many excellent foster homes.

Nevertheless, Gordie had the bad luck of being placed in a series of the bad kind of foster homes. Each family met his needs in terms of food, clothing, shelter, and medicine, but they didn't meet his biggest need: love. He became very shy and quiet, so much so that the social workers who visited and gave reports on Gordie said he was "slightly mentally disabled." (Actually, that's a modern expression; in those days they used to say "mentally retarded.") He would never do well in school. At least that's what they said.

Gordie was about six years old when a very fine young couple came to see him. A niece of theirs who used to baby-sit Gordie had told them about him. They had no children of their own and wanted very much to adopt someone. It didn't seem to matter whether it was a girl or boy, or what age he or she was. They just wanted a child. Their names were Paul and Johanna Webster.

For some reason, the moment Gordie saw them he smiled. And what a smile he had! In fact, someone had said that if you got past Gordie's shyness, his smile would make him your friend for life. And it was true. The problem was that he hardly ever smiled. He seemed so sad that when he *did* smile, it really took you by surprise—kind of like the sun suddenly breaking through on a cold and cloudy day.

Well, the sun broke through on the Websters that day, and within six weeks Gordie was theirs. They were thrilled! But Gordie wasn't too impressed.

After all, he had seen several homes in his short life, and this was just another one. But it wasn't long before he began to see big differences—like lots of *new* toys, *new* clothes, a bright room of his own, excellent food, and lots of love.

Strangely enough, it was the love that he disliked. He disliked it because it scared him. He'd never experienced it before and thought that his new parents were trying to get too close to him. He had lived all his life surrounded by people but hugged by no one. Even when he was in a room of people he felt distant from them. After six years of this, he had become very used to isolation. He created his own little world and resented anyone who tried to break into it. I know it sounds a little strange, but when his parents tried to get too close he felt somehow like they were trying to take his clothes off. Love made him feel weak and naked.

So, instead of receiving and returning love, he learned how to use love. His parents were so eager to please him, to make up for all the love he had never had and the love they had never given to a child before, that they overdid it. If he broke a toy in anger, they'd say, "Oh, the poor boy, he's been so neglected in his life he just doesn't know how to behave." If he yelled at his mom or dad, they'd say, "Well, that's all he's seen these past six years. Who can blame him?" If he refused to eat, his mom would say, "That's okay, Gordie, what *would* you like? Mommy will make it for you." What Gordie wanted, Gordie got. For every failure of his, they would make an excuse. For any damage he caused, they would pay. In no time at all Gordie was ruling his house. He became a tyrant.

As time went on and the years passed, Gordie grew to despise his parents. Rather than being grateful, he became hateful. He had no respect for them because he could manipulate them. Isn't it interesting that we respect people who hold us responsible for our actions, and we have no respect for those who say, "Do what you want; I don't care"? Maybe that's the point: care. If parents really care for you, they won't let you do whatever you want to do. Instead, they'll insist that you do what's *right* for you. And doing what's right is often tough and unpleasant (like homework). On the other hand, parents who let you get away with murder are doing you no favor at all. They're merely getting you out of their hair.

Years ago I heard a radio talk-show where the host asked his teenaged audience what they thought about curfews. (A *curfew* is a time set by your mom or dad for you to get home after being out somewhere—say it's 6:00 P.M. If you come home at 6:30, you're in big trouble!) I thought the callers would all say, "We *hate* curfews!" Boy, was I surprised. Those who had curfews said, "My curfew means my parents care about me." Those who didn't have curfews said, "I wish I had one. Not having one means my parents don't care." You see, there's something inside all of us that says love, to truly be love, sometimes has to be tough.

You would think that school might have had a positive effect on Gordie's attitude. After all, teachers are tough, right? Well, yes and no. Gordie had become such a skilled manipulator that he managed to get his own way much of the time. He had very few friends, however. Other kids have a way of spotting a guy like Gordie. The friends he *did* have were all very much like him. They formed their own sort of tyrants' club.

As you've probably already guessed, Gordie never completed his education. He dropped out after two years of high school. He started drinking heavily, got a girl pregnant, ran away, and unfortunately ended up doing a seven-year term in jail for bank robbery.

Now, I can hear you saying, "Wait a minute, Uncle Bob! You said Gordie was a chum of yours. How come? Were you a tyrant too?" No, I hope not. The reason I called him a chum was that we played on the junior football team together. Gordie was very big and athletic. And in a setting (like a football team) where there were very strict rules and no foolishness was allowed, Gordie became a very nice guy. We played next to each other on the defensive line and became very dependent on each other in game situations. He always played hard and well.

That's why it's so sad that Gordie became such a failure in the game of life. If he had had rules when he was young, he would have had freedom when he was old. Fortunately, he did finally encounter some rules—in prison. And they changed his life.

Today at lunch he told me about prison. It was everything his homelife had not been. The guards and his fellow prisoners didn't let him get away with anything. He was forced to obey. At first he rebelled, but he found that rebellion only increased his pain. He tried to manipulate, but that didn't work either (there's nobody like prison inmates to make life rough for a manipulator). Finally he gave in. He started to behave. He learned computers in the prison school. And he even got a university business degree! He worked out in the prison gym and became huge. He even went to chapel! Gordie became a new person.

Today he has a very good job with a computer company. He has two hundred people working for him, and most of them say he's the nicest and fairest boss they've ever had. "But," they're quick to add, "he's tough. Very tough!"

I'm glad I had lunch with Gordie. It reminded me of a most important thing: your attitude can make or break you. Whether you're young (like you are) or old (like me), attitude means everything. How you treat the world will determine how the world treats you. Most of Gordie's fellow prisoners felt that the world owed them. Gordie learned that the opposite is true: we owe the world.

I'll never forget President Kennedy in his inaugural speech saying, "Ask not what your country can do for you; ask what you can do for your country." Attitude is everything.

Well, I've got to go now. Believe it or not, I'm hungry again! And Aunt Jenny is calling me to dinner. Say hi to your mom.

Love ya,
Uncle Bob

12

Dear Jess and Kate,

Aunt Jenny and I really enjoyed your last letters—especially the pictures you included. I didn't know that your mom had those old black and white shots of Living Waters Camp. Isn't that a great one with your mom and me and Mickey the bulldog? He was quite the fighter! I'll tell you about him in this letter.

A few letters ago I described the trip to Lake Manitou. I can still taste the dust in my throat, to say nothing of the other stuff I threw up by the side of the road! What a trip it was, and were we ever glad when that adventure was over! But now a new adventure awaited us: getting to know Living Waters Camp.

My first impression was how old the buildings looked. Dad told us they had been built about fifty years before by a health club that believed the salty waters of Lake Manitou had healing powers. They were all lacking paint; in fact, the general color was weather-beaten gray. And they had a sort of wounded look to them. You know that buildings usually have a lot of straight lines, edges, and angles. Not these buildings. They looked soft and wavy. They had the slightly stooped back and rounded shoulders of an old grandfather. If you looked at a roof, you'd see that it drooped in the middle.

A door would hang crookedly; a window frame would bend out from the building slightly—the effect of years of warping by the wind, rain, snow, and sun. And the foundations seemed to have sunk into the ground. I remember thinking that Living Waters Camp looked like it was growing *from* the ground rather than having been built *on* it. It was like an old tree calling out for you to climb its branches. I could hardly wait to begin exploring!

Let me tell you about our room. Mr. Fenton Harper, the caretaker, took us to a building that once had been the hotel for the health club. As we walked over to it, he told us to make sure to open the windows and check for dead mice. "We used to have rats, but the heat of the past few summers either scared 'em all away or killed 'em," he said. "The mice haven't done much better," he added. "Thank God," said Mother.

Our room was on the side of the hotel facing the lake. The door was at ground level (more like a motel room), and there were two windows on either side. It took Mr. Harper several tries before he found the right key; and when he did, the door refused to open any more than halfway. "No problem," he said, as he pulled a small can of oil out of his pocket. "These things are pretty rusty. It's the salt air, you know." He worked away at the reluctant lock for a moment or two, finally succeeding in "unstucking" it, as he called it. Next he had to give two or three full-bodied shoulder thumps to the door, and we were in. "Air's kinda dead in here," he said as he opened the windows. "Don't forget to close 'em at night—mosquitoes, you know." With that he left us, calling as he rounded the corner, "If there's any problem you know where to find me." Well, we didn't know, but we'd find out if we had to. The important thing was that we were here, and this would be home for the next month.

The room was not nearly as impressive as the sudden curl on Mother's lip. It was about twelve feet long and ten feet wide. There was a metal double bed frame (without mattress) for Mother and Dad and a built-in wooden bunk bed for your mom and me. There was a worn-out piece of carpet on the floor ("Ugh! We've got to get rid of that," said Mother) and about two hundred dead flies on the windowsills. Oh yes—there *was* a dead mouse, so flat and dried out it looked like it had been mummified. I shoved it out the door with my foot. As Dad went to find some mattresses, the rest of us went back to the car to get our bags. We dropped them outside the room, and Mother went looking for a broom and a pail of water. She wasn't about to have us living in that room until it was clean. Personally, I thought it was fine the way it was, but mothers are like that, right?

While our parents were out looking for things, your mom and I went exploring. As we went around the building to find the main entrance, we saw a strange sight. It was an old green Jeep pulling what looked like a wooden raft along the ground. The raft had several garbage cans on it. To my amazement, the person driving the Jeep appeared to be only three or four years older than I was. He stopped right beside us and said, "Want a ride?"

"Sure," I answered. As we ran around to the passenger side he said, "No! Not here—back there, with the barrels in the stone-boat." Without asking any questions we scrambled onto the "stoneboat" (I *loved* that name!), and the boy drove off with us in tow. We didn't know where we were going, we didn't know our driver's name, and we didn't care—this was fun!

In just a few minutes we were covered with dust as the stoneboat scraped and bounced along. It took all we had just to stay on it—in fact, your mom fell off once, but quickly caught up and jumped on again. Through the dust and the noise the boy called back, "We're goin' down to the dump. Hold on! It gets kinda bumpy here!" With that, we came over a ridge about a half-mile from the camp and scraped and slid down a very rough path to a smelly, smoky pit full of garbage.

Stopping the Jeep, our new friend jumped out and asked me to help him unload the garbage. We rolled the barrels on their bottom edges off the stoneboat and over to the edge of the pit. Then we carefully tipped them until the contents slid out. As we were loading them back onto the stoneboat, the boy smiled at us and said, "My name's Willard; what's yours?" With that formality over, he hopped back in the Jeep, your mom got into the passenger seat, and I stayed on the stoneboat. My job now was to balance the empty barrels and myself on this wooden raft as Willard drove back to the camp at a much higher rate of speed. We had to stop twice—once to retrieve a barrel that bounced off, and once to give me time to catch up after falling off! I was scraped, bruised, and happy. I was also envious—I wanted to drive that Jeep!

When we got back to the camp, we saw another cloud of dust over by the dining hall. This, we discovered as we drew near, wasn't caused by another Jeep and stoneboat, but by a dog fight! Willard jumped out of the Jeep and yelled, "Attaboy, Mickey! Keep it up, boy! Good job, fella!" I had to run up to Willard's side before I could see what was going on in all the dust. What I saw amazed me!

Whirling around and around, as if he were a hairy top, was a huge brown dog. Hanging on by his teeth to the big dog's cheek was a much smaller, short-haired dog. His name was Mickey. He was a bullterrier and was having the fight, and ride, of his life.

The big dog was so huge and so powerful that he had Mickey flying around with his short body parallel to the ground. Occasionally the big dog would snap his head (and Mickey) to the ground, where Mickey hit the dirt like a sack. Then the big dog would throw his head in an arc up to the sky, where Mickey would fly like Superman. But Mickey kept his teeth firmly clamped on the big dog's cheek. He refused to let go.

We could see that the big dog was tiring. A few times he would just lie on the ground panting. Lying beside him in the dirt, also panting, was Mickey, his teeth still fixed on the other's cheek. After these rests, the big dog would start his shaking and whirling all over again, but Mickey hung on. Finally the big dog had had enough. He lay down in defeat. After a few moments Mickey, whose eyes had been squinted shut during the violence of the fight, opened them. I saw a gleam of victory. He slowly released his hold on the big dog's face, stood up, shook himself (creating his own minor dust storm) and walked slowly and triumphantly away.

Willard ran over to Mickey and picked him up. "Great job, Mick! Good goin', boy," he said, as Mickey licked Willard's chin. "That's my dog, ya know," he said to me. "I've never seen him lose a fight. They can't beat Mick's cheek-hold." Then, putting Mickey down and running toward a small shed that displayed an old sign saying CANTEEN, he cried, "C'mon! Let's go get a pop!" We left your mom behind in the dust.

"Hi, Mr. Skowcroft!" Willard greeted the man stacking heavy wooden cases full of bottled pop. "Could Bobby an' me have a Coke?" he asked. "Sure thing, Willard. You'll pay me later, right?" "Yep, sure will. Here, Bobby, have a Coke." I took the bottle and drained it. It was warm, but it was wet. It was one of the best drinks I've ever had in my life—not just because my throat was as dry as the ground, but because it had been given to me by a new friend, a boy I felt I'd always known. We clinked our bottles together and laughed for pure joy. I'd made a friend for the rest of my life.

Over the next few days Willard and I spent every waking moment together. We explored the buildings, hiked through the hills, and even swam in the lake. I'll tell you more about this in future letters. But before I close this letter, I want to share something about friendship.

It has been almost forty years since Willard and I met. We are still friends—*best* friends, in fact. I've learned something about best friends, however. I can count my best friends on one hand—I have only four (and the *best* best friend is your Aunt Jenny). And you know what? It seems that the most "best" friends any of us can handle is no more than four or five. You'll have lots of friends over the years, but be aware that there will be just a few "Willards" in your life. Willard was someone for whom I had an instant liking. We had a "chemistry," you might say. And that chemistry is just as real today as it was back in 1954.

When you feel lonely from time to time, and maybe a little friendless, just remember this: it's taken me all my life to find and develop a lasting bond with four people. When I'm with any one of them, I feel richly blessed. Sometimes we don't see each other for years; but when we do meet, we pick up where we left off. Best friends may be few and far between—but they're forever.

I'll write again soon.

Love ya,
Uncle Bob

13

Dear Jess and Kate,

A few letters ago I was so angry at what Adam Gibson had done to Rocky that I wanted to kill him. Remember? Well, in spite of our Sunday school teacher's wise words, I *still* wanted to kill him—or hurt him some way. Just to get even. (Now, I know, and so do you, that I didn't really *intend* to kill him; I just *wanted* to. Justice demanded that he suffer for what he'd done.) Little did I know that my hatred for Adam would change. I really didn't expect what happened the day I went to find him and punch his nose in.

Before I tell you about that meeting, however, I should bring you up to date on Rocky's condition. The morning after his accident, his left hind leg was so swollen it looked as though it might burst. Mother was so concerned that she called Farmer

Findley. Farmer Findley was no doctor; in fact, he hadn't ever gone to school. But he was well known in our area as someone who could tend a sick animal better than anyone in town. I had been to his farm a couple of times with Mother to pick up some eggs and a few pies (Mrs. Findley was a very kind person with a heart for needy families), and both times I was amazed at what I saw.

Farmer Findley raised bulls—huge, mean-looking, Black Angus bulls. He kept them in a massive corral made of telephone poles! When I was there he had five bulls inside, all of different ages and sizes. To keep them from fighting he had several smaller corrals within the big corral; each bull had his own enclosed space. The biggest of them all was a midnight-black creature called Horner.

Three things struck me as I looked at Horner. First was his hugeness, second was the mean-looking gleam in his eyes, and third was the huge silver ring in his nose. Farmer Findley told me that Horner weighed over two thousand pounds (which made him one of the biggest Black Angus bulls in the west). He was very, very nasty, said Farmer Findley. When I came close to his corral, he charged and hit the telephone poles with such force that the ground shook! But he'd let Farmer Findley right into his corral. He would allow the farmer to take hold of the ring in his nose, and he'd go wherever Farmer Findley led him. I learned later that a bull's nose is very tender (like ours), and just a small twist of the ring would make him turn wherever Farmer Findley wanted him to go. I saw this happen once and was very impressed with the power Farmer Findley had over Horner just by twisting that ring. Horner followed the farmer like a small dog on a leash.

Farmer Findley's reputation as an animal doctor had very little to do with bulls, however. Over the years he had cured all kinds of horses, cows, sheep, goats, dogs, cats, and even an elephant (from a visiting circus). One of his most remarkable cures concerned Annie Morrison's goat. Miss Morrison was a retired schoolteacher who lived alone on a small farm not far from Findley's. She came rushing to Farmer Findley late one Saturday afternoon and breathlessly told him that Elma the nanny goat had just broken her right rear leg. "She's in awful pain, Farmer Findley," she said. "It's pointing straight sideways and is almost broken right off. Please help!" So, picking from the shelf an old whiskey bottle with a rag stuffed in the top, Farmer Findley rushed over to Annie Morrison's farm.

Elma was in sad shape. Farmer Findley quickly decided that if he tried to straighten the leg it might break right off, just as Annie had suggested. It was broken just above the knee and pointed at a right angle sideways. So he settled on a very remarkable cure. First he took the rag out of the whiskey bottle and poured some of its smelly contents right on the break. Elma gave a few bleats, but didn't complain further. Then he took two straight pieces of wood, each about eight inches in length. He nailed them together at right angles and very gently strapped it to Elma's leg. He poured more of the liquid on the break, then wrapped the entire leg in long white strips of an old sheet that Annie supplied. A week later Elma was walking, running even (!) around the yard on three legs. The broken leg was nearly mended—pointing straight sideways. She lived for years, but always appeared to be signaling a right turn! She became a real attraction; in fact, people used to drive from miles around just to see Farmer Findley's artwork. Both Elma and Annie were very pleased.

When Farmer Findley came to our place he had only one medicine, a whiskey bottle with a rag stuffed in the top. He bent over Rocky's box and very gently examined his swollen leg. Pulling the rag out of the bottle, he poured some of that evil-smelling stuff over the wounded limb as the room filled with the rank odor. Then he took a small pocketknife and made a small cut on the bottom of Rocky's foot. A sudden geyser of blood gushed out. Farmer Findley massaged the leg while less and less blood flowed; then he poured more of the liquid on the incision. He wrapped the wound in strips of cloth that Mother gave him. "Should be okay in a few days," he said, and without any further comment he started for the door.

My curiosity overcame me and I blurted out, "Farmer Findley, what's that stuff in the bottle?" He pulled it out of his coat pocket and answered, "This? Oh, it's a little family secret. It's called

'Findley's Liniment'—cures everything from chest colds to broken legs." And with a smile he asked, "Would you like me to leave some?" At a nod from Mother, he left the bottle on the table. Findley's Wonder-Working Liniment. I still think it's the best cure-all in the history of medicine.

Just as the "doctor" had said, Rocky was fine in a few days. Before we knew it he was running around the house, as playful as ever. He was cured. But my anger at Adam wasn't. I still wanted justice.

I hadn't seen Adam since the "accident." A day or two after Rocky seemed completely well, I decided to ride my bike to Adam's shed. As I rode I imagined the conversation and the fight I was about to have. I would accuse him of deliberately leading Rocky in front of the car. He would deny it. "Oh yeah?" I would ask. "Oh yeah," he would answer. "Oh yeah?" I would ask again, this time shoving him in the chest. "Oh yeah," he would answer, shoving me back. Then I would shove him; he would shove me; and we would wrestle, punch, kick, gouge, and hit. At least, this is how fights usually went. My problem was that I'd never been in a fight before. I was nervous, and my stomach told me so as I rode. But I was more angry than I was nervous, so I kept pedaling.

As I approached Adam's aunts' house I became even more nervous, not about fighting but about being seen by the witches. I knew they weren't really witches—but one mustn't be careless, right? This was really the first time I'd been close to their house. It looked haunted, and I suddenly felt very scared. Fortunately, no one seemed to be home. I dropped my bike on its side in the driveway and tiptoed past the house on my way to Adam's shed. At the moment my anger had completely disappeared. I just wanted to avoid those evil aunts.

Rounding the back corner of the house, I suddenly came face to face with both of them! They were gardening, and they looked up at me with startled and angry faces. My heart was in my mouth as one hissed, "Who are you? What do you want?" For a second or two my mouth moved, but my voice escaped me. Finally I stammered, "I—I came to see Adam, ma'am." Motioning toward the shed, she said, "Do as you please. The little brat is playing sick."

I ran to the shed, burst through the door, and closed it, relieved to put those dreadful old women behind me. This kind of approach to the shed had not been in the plan. I *had* planned to throw rocks at it and challenge Adam out to mortal combat. But here I was, trembling and thankful to be in the shed, having escaped a witch's curse. What I saw then shocked me more than I can say.

There was Adam, curled up under an awful old blanket on a mattress on the dirt floor, shivering as though it were the middle of winter. His hair was plastered to his forehead with sweat; his teeth were chattering; and his skin looked yellow. He turned his eyes toward me, but they were filmy and unfocused. Just as I was about to say something, he broke into the worst cough I'd ever heard. I knelt beside him and put my hand on his head. It was boiling! He looked like he was about to die.

Without saying anything I rushed out the door, not even caring if the witches were still there (they weren't). As I got to my bike I saw an old truck rattling up the dusty road toward me. Praise be! It was Farmer Findley! I ran out into the road and frantically flagged him down. He stopped and asked, "What's the matter, boy?" I quickly answered, "It's Adam, sir! I think he's dying! He needs help!" Without any further explanation I led him to the shed, where he quickly assessed the situation and said, "Let's take him to Mrs. Findley. The poor boy's almost a goner."

We carried Adam to the truck and laid him down in the back. I sat with him and put his head in my lap to lessen the bumps as the truck moved along. Shortly we arrived at Findley's farm.

In no time Mrs. Findley had Adam bathed and lying under two feather blankets. Then Farmer Findley came in with a whiskey bottle and pulled the rag from the top. "Here, Bobby, rub this on Adam's chest," he ordered. For the next ten minutes I rubbed the foul-smelling Findley's liniment on my mortal enemy's coughing chest. As I did so he looked up at me, his eyes clearing, and whispered hoarsely, "That stuff stinks!" My eyes teared, not at the vile fumes, but at the overwhelming joy of knowing that Adam was going to live.

Adam stayed under the Findleys' care for a long time. Every day I came to visit, and every day I rubbed some liniment onto his chest. One day I even brought Rocky to visit. As Rocky licked Adam's face I looked at the old whiskey bottle on the bed-table. Findley's Wonder-Working Liniment had truly done wonders. It had saved my enemy's life, just as it had Rocky's, who, by the way, was kissing Adam's face!

Adam became, and still is, one of those best friends I told you about in my last letter. We had lots of adventures together. I'll tell you about some of them sometime.

I'll write again soon.

Love ya,
Uncle Bob

14

Dear Jess and Kate

I'm sitting here by the fire again, thinking about summer. I've told you about our first summer at Living Waters Camp (and I'll tell you much more about it soon), but remember several letters ago when I told you about Rainbow Village on Manitoulin Island? You may recall that I was twelve and your mom ten when we first visited that fantastic place. And we loved it! Not that we didn't enjoy Living Waters—but after two summers in that arid dust bowl, our first summer at Rainbow Village nearly blew us away with its beauty. It was absolutely gorgeous, peaceful, and spiritual.

Spiritual? What do I mean by that? Well, let me tell you about it.

Have you ever walked through a field of tall grass with the soft fragrance of the wildflowers tickling your nose, the grasshoppers and crickets buzzing in your ears, the sun warming your hair, and you just suddenly want to run, jump, and roll around in it all? Have you ever looked at a little baby, and, as it grasps your finger in its little hand, your heart suddenly seems to swell with such a warm feeling that you're not sure if your chest can hold it in? Have you ever watched a movie or read a book where something so totally sad happens that you feel your heart will break? If you've experienced anything like this, you know what *spiritual* means.

The spiritual part of us never grows old. It's the part that sings, laughs, cries, and rages in us. It's the part that loves and hates. In fact, it's much more than a "part" of us—it's the foundation on which our lives are built.

To put it another way, our spirit or "soul" is the reason we do what we do. And it helps us know of the rightness or wrongness of what we do. For example, I remember that before Dad left us, he was the one I most wanted to show off to when I was hitting a ball, running a race, or lifting a heavy rock. He was my reference point. If he approved of what I did, I was happy. If he disapproved, I was unhappy. Just knowing that he was watching me swing the bat, run, or lift, gave me all the motivation I needed to do it well. My performance was "fueled" by his interest. His participation—just watching me—seemed to be all the reason I needed to do my best.

Maybe the simplest way to put it is this: the outside part of you (the athlete, the student, the explorer) serves the inside part of you (the dreamer, the thinker, the lover). What you are on the outside reflects what you are on the inside. The "child" on the surface seeks to please the "Father" beneath the surface. Or, as the Bible puts it, "As a man thinks in his heart, so is he."

I've already told you about Jackson's Point and all the fun your mom and I had there. I haven't told you about the places I used to go all alone. I loved being alone. *Aloneness* is not *loneliness.* Grown-ups call it *solitude,* and it's a wonderful thing; or at least it *can* be. During those alone times your spirit really surfaces.

There were three places I especially treasured. One was a lonely meadow about a mile from Rainbow Village. Another was Slessor's barn, an old weather-beaten building that didn't house animals anymore but was used for storing thousands of bales of hay. The third place was my little fishing dinghy, anchored hundreds of yards offshore, on Lake Kagawong.

To get to the meadow I had to climb through, or over, several split-rail fences, and walk through about six or seven fields of cows. I'm not sure exactly why the fences were called *split-rail*—but they were long pieces of wood that looked like they had been split, rather than sawed, from larger pieces. They were piled on top of each other in a zigzag way, and stakes tied at the ends by wire kept them together.

Here's a rough picture:

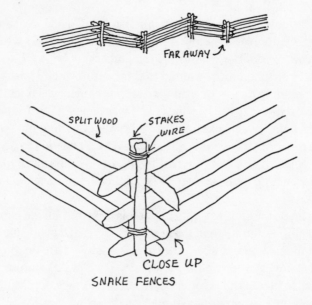

FAR AWAY

SPLIT WOOD   STAKES   WIRE

CLOSE UP

SNAKE FENCES

As you can see, the zigzag made the fences look like a long snake when they stretched for a few hundred feet or so. That's why they were also called *snake fences*. Manitoulin Island is the only place I've seen them, but they've got to be the most environmentally friendly fences anywhere. Their natural wood color (weathered gray), their lack of nails and cement, and their flexibility (they easily follow the contours of the land) make them look as if God had placed them there. It's as if they are growing out of the ground.

Getting over the fences was easy. Getting through the fields of cows wasn't. Not because of the cow pies, but mainly because of the cows! Every time I'd enter one of those fields (always at the far end, away from the cows) they'd come walking, sometimes running, over to me. At the time I thought they were attack cows! Today, of course, I realize that they thought I was the farmer, about to lead them back to their cozy barn. But, being young, small, and no farmer, I thought my life was in the balance. So every field-crossing saw me running back and forth at top speed—just as if I were carrying a football through the defensive line of the Pittsburgh Steelers!

At the far edge of the last field was a forest. It was a dark green forest, with lots of very tall, stately oak trees. I'd climb over the fence, look back victoriously at the attack cows, and enter these most marvelous woods.

Depending on where I'd leaped the fence (the location being the furthest point from the killer cows!), I would find my way to a path that once had been an old cart trail. It was a wonderful path, winding through huge oaks and filtered sunshine. The canopy of leaves above provided the filter, and it was so effective that very little undergrowth grew between the trees. There was a hush beneath those trees. Even the singing of the birds and the buzzing of the insects seemed muted. It felt like a living cathedral.

After I walked for five minutes, the forest floor began to descend. Then with five more minutes of walking downhill, the path led to a diamond-shaped meadow that always surprised me with its sudden brightness. It was breathtaking. The light was overwhelming, and so was the action! Birds seemed to be singing and swooping everywhere; the insects made such a commotion with their buzzing that they sounded like a town-hall meeting; and the wildflowers formed a reckless blaze of color. The subdued, regal rules of the forest gave way to a youthful party of sight, sound, and smell in that little meadow. In the forest I felt like the only child among a group of adults. In the meadow I felt like I'd found the playground.

Its size was roughly the same as a football field, and right in the middle was a large boulder. When I say large I mean *big!* It was about twice as tall as I was and fifteen or twenty feet across its flat top. Climbing onto it wasn't easy; but once I was up there, I could see for miles!

The meadow was on the side of a huge forested hill that dropped suddenly at that point. The tops of the trees on the far side seemed below me when I sat on top of Lone Eagle (as I called the rock). Beyond the trees I could see across a very wide plain all the way to a lake called Mindemoya. In the middle of that lake, on the horizon, I could see an island that the locals called Treasure Island. I always wanted to get there but never did—although it figured largely in some of my daydreams as I sat on Lone Eagle.

More than daydreaming, I used to do a lot of thinking on that rock. The summer I turned twelve, my first thoughts there were about my dad. He had left us long ago, and I still wasn't used to his absence. I missed him.

I was getting over blaming myself. I knew it wasn't my fault he'd left—at least I *thought* so. I think I'd gotten over most of my anger. Then again, maybe I hadn't—maybe I had just redirected my anger. I found that I was very jealous of any child anywhere who had both his parents. Whenever I met a friend's father my face would blush, my heart would ache, and my stomach would cramp. I was both attracted to and repelled by two-parent homes. I wanted Dad back. Oh! How I wanted him back.

It's not fair, I remember thinking on Lone Eagle. *Why should Olaf and Molly have their dad? Why should Darryl have his dad? How come the whole world has dads and I have none?* I couldn't answer these questions. So I did what most people do when they meet an unanswerable question head-on: I blamed God.

This brought relief. It's great to be able to finally blame someone for your hurt. I reveled in it. *I'll never go to church, that's for sure,* I thought. *And all that religious stuff at Living Waters Camp, it's all phony, garbage!* The fact that Dad had been so religious when he was at Living Waters had always amazed me. When he was there he never drank, never abused Mother or your mom and me. He used to sing the hymns loudly with a wonderful smile on his face and intensity in his eyes. He never missed a meeting. It was almost as if he exchanged one addiction (alcohol) for another (religion) each summer. But when we got back to Butte, he very quickly fell back into his old habits.

If God exists and loves us, I thought, *then He wouldn't let this happen.* So I concluded that either God didn't exist, or else He was not as loving and powerful as everyone said He was. At best, He liked playing games with people's lives—*my* life! I felt victimized by heaven. I decided to get even. I wouldn't believe anymore. I'd become an atheist.

As I left Lone Eagle that day I felt very free—or maybe *reckless* is a better word. Until that day I'd always believed in God. But now that my earthly father had deserted me, I felt very satisfied in choosing to desert my Heavenly Father. Fair is fair, right?

Suddenly, with God out of my life, I sensed the excitement of living without rules, without having to answer to anyone, without having to please anyone but myself. I felt almost drunk with opportunity.

This spiritual decision had immediate results. I became impossible to live with. If Dad could break all the rules, so could I. If Dad could hurt Mother and my sister, so could I. If Dad could so easily shove God out of his life, so could I. For the next few weeks I made life a living hell for Mother and your mom. But then something happened to me at Slessor's barn. More about that in the next letter.

I love you a lot!
Uncle Bob

15

Dear Jess and Kate,

In my last letter I had left God behind at Lone Eagle and was now a reckless, hell-raising atheist. Mother couldn't believe the transformation. I was surly and disobedient, selfish and demanding. The strange thing is that this was supposed to be freedom, and freedom meant happiness, right? Well, I was miserable—maybe because being free from God also meant being free from feeling His care. Or perhaps no rules meant no meaning. I don't know. Maybe it wasn't anything theological. Maybe it was growing pains. All I know is that I wasn't happy. And I would have stayed that way, I'm sure, if it weren't for an adventure in which I could have died. Here's what happened.

Rainbow Village was right on the shore of Lake Kagawong, and you got there either by boat or by taking a narrow gravel road that followed the shoreline and wound right around the lake. It was called Perivale Road and was just wide enough for two cars to pass. It led through the forests and fields that bordered the lake.

About three hundred yards north of the entrance to Rainbow Village, on the other side of the road, was Slessor's barn. It was surrounded by a ripening field of hay and looked like a big gray ship sailing on a gray-green sea. Your mom and I had been told by some of our friends at Rainbow Village that it was haunted. A farm worker had fallen and broken his neck in the barn some forty years earlier, and some folks said his spirit still wandered the stalls.

Now that I was an atheist, I didn't have to worry about spirits. By definition, God is the greatest Spirit. If you don't remove the spirits next in line to God, they would replace Him, and God would exist again. By making that one decision on Lone Eagle to stop believing in God, I had really simplified my life. From now on I had nothing to fear, and the meaning of life was simple: look out for Number One. Me. As for ghosts haunting barns, forget it! Who believed in that hogwash? Not me. I was above such stuff.

Mind you, I just happened to have your mom with me when I went to explore the barn for the first time. It wasn't that I was scared. Well, I *was* scared, but not because of ghosts; my fear was of the unknown. You know what it's like to visit some spooky or mysterious place for the first time. Even going to school the first day of the schoolyear is scary. Who knows what your classmates or your teacher will be like? Having someone you know with you when exploring the unknown gives you courage. You may be just as scared as if you were alone, but for your companion's sake (or is it pride's sake?) you try to appear to be brave. And, in a strange sort of way, just trying to look courageous makes you act courageously (even though you may be shaking on the inside).

Perivale Road took a sharp turn left about two hundred yards north of the driveway to Rainbow Village. At the turn, the trees that lined both sides of the road gave way to several hundred acres of hayfields. In the middle of the field closest to the road was Slessor's barn. As we waded through the waist-high grass, the first thing I noticed about the barn was its size. It appeared to be about seventy feet high and two hundred feet long. It had a peaked roof and an L-shaped extension at the end farthest from the road. A large ramp made of grass-covered earth led up to the huge entrance doors. The doors were open, and birds were flying in and out.

As we approached, I noticed that the grass at the bottom of the ramp was just as tall as the grass around the barn. The barn obviously wasn't being used—at least, no tractors or other farm vehicles had flattened the grass at the entryway this year. In fact, the barn had a deserted look about it. The only action seemed to be the coming and going of the birds. And the barn had a kind of deserted smell about it too. The fragrance was old and musty. Old manure, old hay, old wood, and old dust all combined to make an odor that I could almost touch. It smelled like the old wood on a worn staircase railing feels: smooth. It stroked the senses and almost made me want to purr.

But the barn had a scary look too. It was dark beyond the open door. And the one-inch gaps between the barn boards reminded me of the gaps between pirates' teeth. The wind whistled through these cracks so that the barn sounded alive as it moaned and groaned. It was almost ghostlike.

Your mom embarrassed me a bit by taking the lead and walking into the barn first. I was just about to suggest that we explore the outside when she went inside. Of course, I quickly followed and played it cool, even though I was quite nervous.

The interior of Slessor's barn was truly one of the most beautiful sights I had ever seen. The beauty started with the hushed and sweet-smelling atmosphere—it had an instant snugness and coziness about it. Then there were those cracks between the barn boards (or slats). Each slat revealed a narrow strip of the bright blue light outside, and it streamed in, creating gorgeous rays in the fine hay-dust that constantly filled the air inside the barn. By the way, I was told later that those slats were placed apart purposely, so that the wind would blow through the barn to keep it well ventilated and the hay dry.

Adding to the beauty were the huge beams that made up the basic structure of the barn. They were massive trees that had been roughly squared and cut to fit together. What amazed me about the fit was the use of large *wooden* spikes (or dowels) and heavy iron braces to hold those beams together. Even though the barn was old, it had a very secure strength about it that gave me the feeling that I could survive *anything* in there—earthquake, hurricane, or flood.

Then there were the things you'd expect to see: built-in ladders (I wanted to climb them all, and soon did!), pitchforks, boxes of twine, bags of seeds, and a very inviting stack of hay bales (with a wonderful pile of loose hay just below one of the crossbeams). In just a matter of moments I was up one of the ladders and onto that very crossbeam, from which I leaped into the air and fell harmlessly into the pile of hay twenty feet below. For the next hour or so, your mom and I climbed and jumped, climbed and jumped, until, exhausted, we lay on the hay laughing and catching our breath. The thought that we might have slipped and fallen from that crossbeam onto the wooden floor never occurred to us. For one thing, we hadn't slipped, not once. And for another, only adults think about those bad things. We were just having fun. And what fun it was!

After resting a bit, we went through a trap-door down another ladder to the lower level. I got a little scared again, but didn't dare show it because your mom didn't seem nervous at all. We found several animal stalls down there, plus old harnesses, bridles, grooming combs (for horses), and even an ancient saddle that had been chewed by mice. When I pointed this out to your mom she cried, "Mice! You mean there are mice in here? Let's get out now!" Girls! No fear of ghosts, but afraid of mice! Who can figure them out?

Well, it was time to leave anyway. But I intended to come back. And I did—several times over the next week, as a matter of fact.

I've often wondered what drew me to that barn. It was more than beauty, fun, or solitude. I think the appeal was its mixture of security and adventure. The barn was like a father—strong and masculine on the inside, but weathered and leaky on the outside. As a father will challenge you to test yourself against the outside world, so too those flashes of the Manitoulin sky that leaked through the slats spoke to me of the huge world I hadn't yet seen.

And the strength, the security, of the inner barn gave me the foundation I needed to dare to test myself. It was as though a father were saying, "If you hurt yourself, or make a mistake, I'll always be here. You can come back and I'll help you heal, even help you dare again." Maybe this is why I spent so much time lying on the bales or sitting on the beams, thinking about life and what I wanted to be when I grew up. I know this sounds a little strange, but I even found myself *talking* to the barn, as if it had ears and a personality. But I was so inspired there! Slessor's barn comforted and challenged me. Like a father.

There was something motherly about it as well. Sometimes I didn't feel like having an adventure; I just felt like being cozy. I soon discovered that I could shift some of the hay bales around and create an entire room inside the pile. Once I'd made the main room, I created tunnels to other rooms until I had a maze of rooms and tunnels. The really neat thing about it was that when I entered, all I had to do was to pull one bale behind me, closing the entrance, and the whole world could pass by and never know I was inside that huge pile of hay! There was enough light leaking through the cracks between the bales that I could even see where I was going. To read comic books, though, I needed the help of a flashlight. Many times I fell asleep in my cozy home beneath the bales. That's what nearly killed me one stormy day.

It was a great day to be inside my hay bales. The rain was pouring down. The thunder and lightning were so loud and so bright that even some of the adults at Rainbow Village were frightened. Taking Mother's umbrella and wearing one of Uncle Bill's raincoats, I ran to Slessor's barn.

Quickly I took the secret entrance to my room inside the bales. With comic books and flashlight, I was soon secure, dry, and happy. Inside the bales, I saw only slight evidence of the flashing and heard only muffled reminders of the thundering outside. I remember feeling very snug, and, I must admit, a bit smug.

Then there was a most terrible crash that shook the barn and shifted the pile of bales. One or two of them fell on me as my heart leaped. I tried immediately to get out but found my way blocked by other bales that had fallen or shifted. As I blindly pushed and pulled at the bales, making slow progress, I began to smell smoke. Smoke! *Oh no!* I thought, *if there's a fire I'm in trouble!*

By the time I finally escaped from the bales, the barn was full of smoke. In fact, everywhere I looked there were huge sheets of flame! The heat was so intense that I could smell my clothes burning. Where was I to go? What was I to do?

"Oh God! Help me!" I shouted (strange talk for an atheist, right?). In desperation I tried running through the flames, only to turn back because of the heat. When it looked as though all was lost, I suddenly remembered the trap-door!

I wish I could finish the story, but at this point I'll have to stop because Aunt Jenny is calling. I'll continue the story next letter. Sorry to keep you hanging!

We sure love you both!
Uncle Bob

16

Dear Jess and Kate,

Hi! How's it going? Your mom called a few days ago and said you were really antsy waiting for this letter. She even said you wanted me to phone and tell you how I escaped the fire in Slessor's barn! Sorry! Maybe I should have written an extra-long letter last time. But now you can relax, because here is part two of the story.

As I said in the last letter, I was surrounded by flames. Every moment they were growing taller and hotter as the dry hay ignited all around me. The smoke was so thick that I threw myself to the floor just to breathe, and even the floorboards were hot! I looked around in desperation, knowing that I had maybe one more minute before dying. At this point the flames were roaring as loudly as a passing freight train, and the floor was vibrating violently. In terror I cried again, "Oh God! Help me!" It was then that I looked across the floor and saw the dim outline of the trap-door leading to the lower level.

I quickly scrambled across the floor on my stomach and grabbed the iron ring handle, not even noticing that it badly burned my fingers. I lifted the door with one hand (in normal times it took all my strength with *two* hands) and fell into the opening headfirst. As I began to fall I grabbed one of the steps of the ladder, and my body crashed against a lower rung. I quickly fell, more than climbed, down the ladder, and crashed onto the dirt floor in a heap. Just as I did, a large flaming timber thudded down beside me in a shower of sparks. This frightened me so that I leaped up and out a window. I rolled and rolled through the grass until I was about a hundred feet away from the barn. Even though I was exhausted, I lifted my head to look. And what I saw amazed me!

The barn was a fireball. The entire structure was blazing with an explosion of flame and billowing smoke. Even at this distance, the heat was nearly more than I could bear. And wonder of wonders—all of this was happening in a driving hailstorm! The hail was slashing down with such volume and force that all the hayfield was flattened, and my skin was smarting with its impact. The lightning was flashing and the clouds were thundering, while the barn was disintegrating before my very eyes.

My body gave me all kinds of conflicting signals as I tried to stand. My eyes were stinging from the smoke and the hail; my skin was boiling from the heat and chilled by the storm; and my stomach, hand, and leg hurt—bad. In fact, as I stood I felt a sudden, sharp pain in my left ankle, so fierce that I instinctively shifted my weight to the right leg. I looked down at my stomach and only then realized that I'd lost my shirt. It hadn't torn off, because my shirt sleeves were bunched around my wrists; it had burned off! My stomach was all blistered. I looked at my left hand, for it had just started to throb, and it too was blistered. Suddenly I felt very weak.

Just then I heard faint voices behind me calling my name. They belonged to Uncle Bill and your mom. I turned to look across the field, and everything started to spin. I fell to the ground; then everything went black.

I don't remember much of what happened next. I was in shock and "came to" and "passed out" several times over the next few minutes. Apparently Uncle Bill and your mom found me lying unconscious in the grass. The heat was so intense even where I lay that they immediately moved me back another hundred feet or so before trying to wake me up. I remember coming to in Uncle Bill's arms as he asked me, "Where does it hurt?" I mumbled something about my stomach, because that's what hurt most. He wrapped me in his coat and carried me back to his cottage at Rainbow Village. All I remember is that every step he took hurt.

The next thing I knew I was lying in a featherbed at Uncle Bill and Aunt Edna's.

Your mom and Mother were there, and so was Doc Ellison, the retired doctor who had been coming every summer for the past thirty years to Bert's Camp (now Rainbow Village). He'd had a family practice in Kansas City and loved to spend his summers on Manitoulin Island. He always had his doctor's kit in his car, a practice he'd followed for decades. As soon as Uncle Bill got back to Rainbow Village with me in his arms, your mom ran over to Ellison's cottage. I had kindly, expert care almost immediately.

I don't remember everything Doc Ellison did. I *do* remember his very gently cleaning me up and then removing the dead skin from my stomach with tweezers. I also remember his saying how important it was to keep me warm, and how lucky I was that the burns were not "third degree." My hand, he said, looked worse than it was. Once he'd cleaned it up, he declared those burns to be second degree as well. After carefully examining my left ankle, he said I had a "severe sprain," and it would be three weeks before I could walk on it without pain. As he wrapped my burns in soft, dry cloth (over some antiseptic pads), he said what concerned him most was my lungs. "He's absorbed a lot of hot smoke," he said to Mother, "and he may find breathing deeply to be a bit painful for a few days. Make sure he does nothing strenuous for a while!" Then, smiling at his own joke (as if I were in any shape to do anything strenuous!), he left, saying he'd check in with me tomorrow, but would be available at any time if needed.

I had a terrible night. My stomach, ankle, and hand all throbbed in time with the pounding inside my head. I had a headache such as I had never before (or since) experienced. It was so intensely painful that I threw up a few times. Several times through the night my vision blurred, and the room started spinning. The slightest movement made my head feel like it would explode.

The next morning, when Mother told Doc Ellison about my headache, he spent a few minutes looking into my eyes with a small light and taking my blood pressure. I was able to answer questions, and when he asked if I'd fallen in the barn, I told him about my fall through the trap-door. "I think you may have suffered a slight concussion, my boy," he said. "Please don't even think of getting out of bed for a few days." I was only too happy to obey. The way I was feeling, I wasn't sure if I'd ever want to get out of bed. He then changed my bandages, gave me a shot with a needle, and left.

The following day I had two unexpected visitors. The first was Mr. John Smelnick, a small red-nosed man who was the fire chief for the Mindemoya, Spring Bay, and Gore Bay area. He wanted to ask me a few questions about the fire. He told me that the main beams of the barn were still standing, although they were badly burned and as black as coal. "It's kind of sad," he said, "that beautiful old barn is nothing but a black skeleton now. Amazing, the power of lightning, eh? Now, son, tell me the story." He listened carefully, making a few notes as I described events as I'd seen them. He wanted to know where the hay bales had been piled in the barn, where the trap-door was, and if there had been any old cans of gasoline or oil lying about. He also wanted to know if the fire had spread gradually or whether it had just "exploded." I told him it had happened as soon as the huge crash had occurred. "No question," he said more to his notebook than to me, "it was a direct hit." He asked a few more questions; then, telling me I was lucky to be alive, left us.

As he left the room I noticed that he walked with a limp. Uncle Bill told me later that Mr. Smelnick had broken his hip and his left leg in four places, years ago, falling through the floor of a burning barn near Gore Bay. "I think his visit today was more to see a fellow barn-fire survivor than it was to get information," he said. I decided right then that when I was better, I would look Mr. Smelnick up and hear his story.

The other visitor that day was Pastor Hummer from the little church in Providence Bay. He knew Uncle Bill and Aunt Edna because they attended his church in the off-season. He had driven by to see what was left of Slessor's barn and had decided to visit Uncle Bill and Aunt Edna on his way home. He hadn't known about my role in the drama. As soon as he heard, he asked if he could visit me in my room.

I was alone when I heard his knock at the door. "Come in," I shouted, and in walked the most unusual-looking preacher I'd ever seen.

He had to duck as he came through the doorway because he was almost seven feet tall! He was wearing a T-shirt, jeans, and sandals. His hair was white-blonde and hung almost to his shoulders, but the top of his head was totally bald and tanned! His nose had about three angles and was pushed to one side of his rugged face. But what really impressed me, apart from his height, was his size. He had huge shoulders, thick arms, and a massive chest. He also had a fairly large stomach, but the rest of him was so big that this large abdomen seemed somehow to be the right size. He told me later that he weighed 310 pounds! He looked like a human version of Slessor's barn.

As he gently shook my bandaged hand it seemed that he was shaking my whole arm. In fact, his hand swallowed not only my hand but also half of my forearm. And how shall I describe his voice? Let me put it this way: Imagine a bass drum talking. Looking me straight in the eye, the bass drum said, "Hi! My name is David Hummer. What's yours?" Before I even gave him my name, I knew I'd found a friend.

Instead of sitting in the chair, he sat on the floor, with his back against the wall. He was so tall that this position put his face on about the same level as mine as I lay with my head propped on two pillows. He listened quietly as I told him my story. When I'd finished he asked one question.

"Did you pray?" he asked.

"What do you mean?" I responded.

"When you were in the middle of the fire—did you pray when you thought you were going to die?"

"Oh. That. Well, er, yeah. Uhmm, no," I lied.

"You mean you didn't shout for God to save you?" he asked.

"I don't remember," I lied again. My atheist pride didn't like where this conversation was heading.

"Boy, that's not like me the time *I* almost died," he said.

"You almost died? From what?" I asked.

"The time I was thrown out of the ring and broke my neck."

"Broke your neck? Out of the ring?"

Before I could ask the next question he answered, "Yeah. The ring, the wrestling ring. I used to be a professional wrestler."

I was hooked. I didn't care if this giant talked to me about God now. I was talking to a *professional* wrestler!

I'll tell you about that conversation in a later letter. In the next letter I'll get back to Rocky's story.

Aunt Jenny sends her love.

I love you too!
Uncle Bob

17   ✍

Dear Jess and Kate,

Hey! Did I ever enjoy the *National Geographic* article you sent me about lightning! Isn't it awesome to think of the power in a lightning strike? Little wonder Slessor's barn burned like a match. And yes, I *am* very fortunate to have survived. Every time I look at the scars on my stomach and hand, I thank God for His protection.

I promised in my last letter to continue Rocky's story. As you remember, he was recovering from being hit by Paul Miller's car. I credited the quickness of his recovery to Farmer Findley's treatment and the generous application of Findley's Liniment to his wounded foot. Within a day or two he was standing and hopping around on three legs. In about a week I saw him gingerly putting his wounded foot down about every third step. Soon he was running and playing as if the accident had never occurred.

After his recovery something funny happened. Paddy David-son came to visit.

Paddy was Rocky's brother. Mayor Davidson had paid Olaf and Molly's mother five dollars for him. That was a lot of money for a dog in those days, but Paddy was the biggest and best-look-ing pup in the litter. I had often seen him playing outside with the mayor's son, Delbert, during those early weeks when Rocky's life was in question. I remember envying Delbert his dog. It seemed that Paddy was everything Rocky wasn't. Where Paddy was big and handsome, Rocky was puny and ugly. Where Paddy was strong and healthy, Rocky was weak and sick. Paddy even had a full-time companion in Delbert, whereas Rocky had to share me with all the chores I had to do around home because of Dad's absence. Paddy was a lucky dog.

The Davidsons lived on the other side of Mother's garden, so I saw Paddy almost every day. As Rocky improved and your mom and I took him outside to play, Paddy would often join us. Dogs are kind of weird when they meet. Humans shake hands or say, "Hi, how's it going?" Dogs sniff each other. Yuck! But that's their way of saying hi. (Give me a handshake any day!)

One such day I learned, in a very important way, that Rocky was something Paddy wasn't. A group of us kids—your mom, me, Delbert Davidson, Darryl Krause, Olaf and Molly, and a few others (*plus* our dogs)—were playing a game of baseball in the field beside the Sandstroms' home. We had just chosen sides (and the dogs had finished sniffing each other!) when Mickey Weller came running across the field with his dog, Duke, to join us. Duke was a Great Dane, and he scared us all. He was so big! Where other dogs would have to jump up on your leg to get your attention, Duke simply had to look you in the eye. His head was just about level with mine (I *was* small for my age), and he outweighed me by at least one hundred pounds. He was the king, or at least the duke, of dogs in our town.

Whenever Duke joined a group he took over. Have you ever noticed what most people do when a dog that scares them comes close? They usually put on an uncertain grin, reach out their hand (as if it's better to sacrifice an arm than a leg), and say, with phony enthusiasm, "Here, boy! Nice dog. Nice dog. How ya doin', fella?" Then, if the dog responds with a growl, they say, "That's okay, boy. I'm not gonna hurt you." In fact, they're afraid the *dog* is going to hurt *them*. This little ritual is almost as weird as dogs saying hi to each other.

For the moment, however, Duke wasn't interested in us kids (we had all shrunk away from him). His first order of business was the sniffing ritual with the other dogs.

The ritual was rather one-sided, mainly because none of the dogs could return the favor due to Duke's height. Rocky, in fact, had to content himself with sniffing Duke's ankle! But this was where Paddy showed us his true colors. When Duke approached him, he turned his backside toward him and wagged it so violently from side to side that his head was actually being hit by his hips! Then, as Duke began the ritual, Paddy rolled over on his back, with his paws hanging limply in the air, and whimpered like a baby. I was shocked. Big, strong, handsome Paddy was a coward. A wimp! I could hardly believe what I was seeing. Even as Paddy was groveling, Rocky was playfully jumping in the air between Duke's front and back legs, trying to nip his stomach. Duke reached down and butted Rocky with his head, sending him tumbling in the grass. But Rocky regained his feet and ran back for more. Meanwhile, Paddy just lay there, whimpering and looking pathetic.

After this sorry performance, Paddy ran as fast as he could across the road and over to his house. The other dogs scattered too. But not Rocky. He wanted to play, and so did Duke! What a sight it was. Perhaps you've seen full-grown dogs playing with pups. They assume puplike behavior and frolic back and forth, looking totally foolish. Well, imagine 180-pound Duke running around and rolling in the grass with 8-pound Rocky! I laughed until my stomach ached!

But that wasn't as funny as what happened the next day. I was out in the backyard hanging some wet clothes on the clothesline for Mother, and Rocky was nosing around the outhouse. (He never seemed to get enough of that place!) I looked up and saw Paddy walking from the Davidson's garden over to our garden. Then he walked along the row of tomatoes toward me. Perhaps he couldn't see me because there was a newly hung sheet on the line between us. He walked right past me and went over to Rocky. Then, as the sniffing ritual began, I noticed that Paddy had something around his neck. As I went over for a closer look I was nearly knocked over by a body flying through the flapping sheets and past me like a bolt out of heaven. "Paddy," the body shouted, "you give that back, right now!" It was Pastor Elkington's wife, Gurnith. Boy, was she mad! Paddy was wearing her husband's clerical collar.

As soon as Paddy saw Gurnith hurtling toward him, he took off like a shot. He ran around the outhouse, then began weaving through the three lines of sheets, towels, jeans, and underwear blowing in the brisk breeze. He thought this was a game! Gurnith, on the other hand, had murder in her eyes. She kept shouting and running, but could never quite catch up to Paddy. I stood there amazed, watching Paddy and the pastor's wife running round and round. Even Rocky was getting a kick out of it, chasing after Mrs. Elkington and nipping at her heels. He thought this was great fun!

Then, out of nowhere Duke appeared, running at full speed toward us. As he galloped across the street toward our yard, Mrs. Elkington and Paddy saw him. Although in full flight themselves, both changed their reasons for running *immediately*. Paddy led the way, changing course for the safety of his house. Mrs. Elkington ran after him, because *her* house was next to the Davidsons'. And Rocky, still thinking this was great fun (especially now that his friend Duke was joining the action), followed at an ever-increasing distance due to his short legs.

Duke quickly outran him and caught up with Mrs. Elkington and Paddy just as the two of them tripped over the chicken wire that Mrs. Martin, the Davidsons' housekeeper, had staked to the row of beans in their garden. Paddy was immediately entangled, while poor Gurnith fell flat on her face in the mud. (The garden had been recently watered.) Mrs. Martin, who had just emerged from the back porch with a load of laundry, screamed, dropped her load, and picked up a broom. She began chasing Duke, who was into his puppy mode of frolic, barking, and jumping back and forth at Paddy. Every time she got close enough she thwacked him with the broom. Once, when Duke was dangerously close to Mrs. Elkington's backside, as she was picking herself up out of the mud, Mrs. Martin took a mighty swing, missed Duke, and hit the poor pastor's wife. She went sprawling back into the mud.

Rocky was in the middle of all this, yipping hilariously, chasing Duke, then Mrs. Martin, then barking at Paddy, and even trying to lick Mrs. Elkington's face as she lay in the row of beans. Mrs. Elkington, by the way, had become *very* angry, mainly because (I think) she was *very* embarrassed. As she got up a second time she was shouting at everyone—Paddy, Duke, Mrs. Martin, and even Rocky! It was not a pretty sight.

Delbert Davidson saved the day. He rushed out the backdoor and rescued Paddy from the chicken wire. He then gave Duke a hoof in the ribs, which sent him away yipping as if he'd broken all his bones. In response to Mrs. Elkington's urgent request, he took the clerical collar from Paddy and gave it to her. Then she stormed off to her house, muttering something about thieves and police.

As everyone disappeared, Rocky sniffed around a bit, then strutted back to our yard as if he had won a great victory. He found me on the ground, where I'd collapsed, weak with laughter.

As I lay in bed that night, still chuckling over what I'd seen, it occurred to me that I'd learned a big lesson from Paddy, Duke, and Rocky. What do you suppose it was?

I'll give you a hint: it had to do with the outward appearance of things, as compared to what's really there on the inside.

Why not write me, and tell me what you think the lesson was. I'll look forward to your letters.

Love you a lot,
Uncle Bob

18

Dear Jess and Kate,

I was just watching a story on TV about the great work being done among poor children by a former bank robber. He's been out of prison for three years and has already established five homes for orphans. He has raised millions of dollars to help kids in the inner cities of America. In the interview portion of the story, he told how his good works had been motivated by sorrow for what he'd done (a bank teller was killed in his last robbery) and by the reaction of the teller's family (they had come to the prison and forgiven him). His story was about the redeeming impact that guilt and forgiveness can have, especially when they produce good works. This reminded me of something that happened to Willard during that summer of '54.

I mentioned before that Living Waters had formerly been a health resort. People believed that the salty water of Lake Manitou had healing powers. They used to come for all sorts of problems, everything from skin diseases to arthritis. Judging from the number of buildings on the site, there must have been a lot of people coming to the resort. I've told you before that the main building was a large hotel-type structure. It was poorly constructed, but it sure had great secret passageways!

Willard showed them to me one rainy day, shortly after Mickey the bulldog's triumph. We had just returned from another stone-boat errand when rain started to pour down. We ran to the nearest doorway, which happened to be the main entrance to the hotel. *Hotel* is not the best word to describe this building; when you hear that word, you think of a building designed to house travelers and tourists. Although hotels differ in their levels of luxury and beauty, they all have certain common characteristics, such as a grand entry and lobby, a registration area, elevators, long, orderly hallways, rooms with beds and toilets, and restaurants. Now, this "hotel" *was* designed (perhaps *intended* is a better word) to house tourists, but that's where any similarity ended. In fact, Willard told me that the caretaker referred to it as the *kennel*. As you may know, a kennel is a doghouse!

In *this* hotel the "grand entry" consisted of a warped screen door and a "lobby" full of smelly piles of limp old cotton-filled mattresses that had to be carried to the rooms (this was one of Dad's jobs). Upon closer investigation I noticed that most of them had suspicious "water" stains. There was no elevator; narrow, creaking stairs got you from floor to floor. The hallways were just wide enough for Dad to walk with a couple of those mattresses on his back. The rooms were more like broom closets, and many of them had no windows! For toilets, there was a row of eight outhouses a hundred feet away (four for men, four for women). To wash up you needed to take a pail to a hand-operated pump another hundred feet past the outhouses, get your water, and then pour it into a chipped enamel basin, generously provided for each room. Most of the men just washed at the pump.

It was the exterior design of the kennel, however, that provided the secret passageways. Whoever had designed the place had apparently been influenced by Chinese pagodas. Have you ever seen a picture of a pagoda? This type of tower is often built over or beside a Buddhist temple. Pagodas usually have several stories that decrease in width as they go up. Each story has an overhanging roof that makes the tower look a bit like an overdecorated wedding cake. Well, the "designer" of the kennel had probably never been to architectural school, and probably had a weak memory as well. The design made the hotel look more like a wooden Christmas tree than a pagoda from the side. Every second story had an overhanging roof that was crudely constructed of plywood and asphalt shingles, denying windows to that floor of rooms. From the front, then, the kennel looked like this:

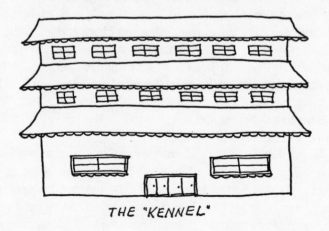

THE "KENNEL"

The overhang, of course, was wasted space (in terms of usable area). But it gave Willard and me hours of fun.

As we ran in out of the rain and the screen door slammed behind us, Willard said, "C'mon, follow me. I want to show you something." He ran up the stairs, and I was close behind. We had to squeeze under and by several walking mattresses (that's how they looked, as a few men were carrying the floppy things up the stairs to the rooms). On the third story Willard led me to a dark corner, where he quickly removed a loose panel. "Quick! In here," he said as he ducked into the darkness. I ducked too and followed him.

As Willard replaced the panel from the inside, my eyes were adjusting to the dim light. We were in a long, triangular tunnel that (I quickly realized) was the inside of one of the pagoda overhangs. It was tall enough, right against the wall, that I could have stood hunched over. In fact, I did exactly that and hit my head on the point of one of the shingling nails sticking through the roof. So I got back on my hands and knees, like Willard. The tunnel seemed to go on forever. Here and there were little cracks, letting in beams of light, which allowed us to see dimly.

Those beams of light, however, weren't as bright as they were on days when the sun was shining. Today the light was gray because of the clouds and rain. The cracks and holes were not only letting dim light in, but water as well. We got both dusty *and* wet as we crawled. The rain drumming on the shingles gave a noisy sound-effect to our exploring. Indeed, it was very much like being inside a drum!

Around the second corner (the passageway had four of them; you guessed that, right?) was a large cardboard box. Willard crawled up to it, turned to me, and said, "I'm gonna show you something secret! If you ever tell—especially my mother—I'm gonna kill ya!" After that threat, I very quickly agreed to keep the secret. Mind you, I was afraid that if I didn't agree, I wouldn't see the treasure, and I loved seeing secret things! So, seeing me nod my head, Willard slowly opened the box. And what do you suppose was in it? Gold? Silver? Jewels? Money? Nope. The box contained a pile of about a hundred comic books!

I was both happy and puzzled to see this huge collection. Happy because I loved to read comics. Puzzled because I didn't know why Willard wanted them kept secret. He saw the question on my face and explained, "My mother thinks comics are bad. She says they're worldly."

"Worldly?" I asked. "What does that mean?"

"Oh, I dunno. They're not the Bible, and they're not about the Bible. So she thinks they're evil. She says anything that isn't religious is worldly."

I wasn't sure I understood, but instead of asking any more questions, I dove into the comics. We each chose one, got as comfortable as we could (it was both dry and well lit there, thanks to a crack that wasn't leaking), and had a delicious three-hour feast of reading.

Over the next few days we took the secret passageway to the comic book treasure-box every afternoon. It took about a week to get through the whole stack.

The following week, on a sunny afternoon, Willard and I were playing catch with an old baseball that had lost its leather covering. Suddenly he said, "Hey, Bobby! Let's go to the Triangle (our code name for the passageway—named after the Bermuda Triangle, no less!). There's something I haven't shown you yet." Willard had a strange look on his face as he led me up the stairs. He looked sort of guilty—like he'd been caught stealing.

We had crawled almost all the way to the comics when Willard stopped. He put his ear to the wall and, more to himself than to me, said, "Yep. She's there." Then very slowly he removed a piece of cardboard that was stuck to the wall with thumbtacks, revealing a dime-sized hole at about eye level. To my amazement, he put his eye to the hole for a moment or two. Then, with a mix of excitement, hush, and guilt on his face, he whispered, "Take a look!"

I felt my face flush immediately as I looked through the hole and saw a stark naked woman! It was Mrs. Reed, Mother's assistant cook, changing into her bathing suit. I recoiled from the sight as if I'd been slapped in the face. I knelt there speechless, my face burning, as Willard quickly put his eye to the peephole.

"Wow! Look at that," he whispered excitedly. "She's huge!" I wasn't sure what he meant by that. I didn't care. All I knew was that I wanted to get out of there fast. Then something terrible happened.

As I scrambled away, Willard lunged to grab my ankle, missed, lost his balance, and fell against the sloping part of the passageway. His face hit several of the exposed nails. As I discovered later, one of them pierced the corner of his eye.

He lay there in agony, both hands clutching his bleeding face, whimpering and groaning pathetically, "My eye! My eye!" At first I didn't know what to do, so I just knelt over him, horrified at what I was seeing. He was cut and/or punctured in several places on the forehead and right temple. As you may know, head wounds bleed a lot. So his face was totally bloody, as were his hands, as he held them over his eye. At this point I started to cry, and my sobs were so pathetic that Willard started comforting me. "Hey, Bobby, it's okay! I'm gonna be okay! Just a bit of blood." But then he groaned again, "My eye! My eye!"

Awkwardly and slowly we made our way down the passageway. Willard was crawling on his knees and left hand, with his right hand tightly pressed against his eye. I saw that this wasn't going to work, so I helped him to lean on my back as I crawled, and that seemed to help. We made a pathetic pair—Willard bleeding all over my jeans, groaning, and gasping, and me blubbering all the way to the hallway. When we got there, I left Willard and ran for help. The first person I met thought *I* had been injured, since I was so covered with blood. But very quickly we had Willard lying in the caretaker's cottage, with people scattering everywhere to find help.

While we waited, one of the women heated some water and began bathing Willard's wounds. But she couldn't get him to move his hand from his eye. Eye wounds are extremely painful, and as Willard was discovering, the only ready relief is pressure on the eye. Soon, however, expert help arrived—the camp nurse and assistant cook, Mrs. Reed.

The hefty woman soon had Willard's eye injury diagnosed—"a slight puncture, and a nasty scratch to the white of the eye." She actually stitched closed some of the bigger head wounds with a needle and thread. She did a good job of patching his eye too—the very eye that only minutes before had been peering into her room from a secret passageway.

Over the next few days, confined to his bed, Willard had a lot of company. As they left, his visitors all said pretty much the same thing. "My! What a fine boy! There he is all banged up, and yet he's so cheery. He cheered *me* up!"

I don't want to be too brainy here—but do you know why Willard was such a comforter to his comforters? I think it was because he knew he'd done wrong by peeping through that hole, and his injuries had been a way of paying the penalty for his crime. I think he also felt somehow that Mrs. Reed's nursing was an act of forgiveness on her part (even though she knew nothing about the peephole). And I *know* (because he told me later) that he had learned a valuable lesson about respecting people's privacy—and we always feel good after we've learned a good lesson. Right?

Anyway, I guess I'm saying that sometimes a little guilt can work wonders, especially when it's mixed with a little pain and forgiveness.

Remember Willard the next time you're punished for doing something wrong. Believe it or not, the short-term pain may bring long-term gain!

Well, I've gone overtime. Time to go. I'll write again next week.

Love ya!
Uncle Bob

19 ☞

Dear Jess and Kate,

Aunt Jenny and I were so excited to read in your last letters about the new bikes! Aren't bikes great? Your mom and I used to *live* on our bikes each summer. They give you a great sense of independence. If you want to go somewhere, you just go, all by yourself. They're great friends. In fact, sometimes when I was riding somewhere I felt that my bike was almost speaking to me. No kidding! You know—the sound of the tires on the road, the rattle of the fenders (but most bikes don't have fenders these days, do they?), the br-r-ring of the chain—all gave my bike a voice, a personality. It was as though motion gave it life. I loved it!

I'm going to tell you the story of how Mother managed to buy those bikes. But before I do, I want to tell you that Aunt Jenny and I were very touched to read your words of thanks. Yes, we *did* send the money to pay for your bikes—but your mom wasn't supposed to tell! We did it, first because we love you, and second because we know that there's never as much money available after a divorce as there is before. In fact, one of the most difficult things about divorce is that there never seems to be enough money. Whether you need shoes, clothes, toys, books, or food, you suddenly discover that you have less money and have to make choices. What you *do* get is often secondhand or of lesser quality. When you look at what some of your friends have, you start thinking you're poor. When we were kids, your mom and I were poor—but we didn't know it. That's where the story of the bikes comes in.

The story starts the winter Dad left us. I've already told you about how difficult it was for me to accept his absence and to do some of the chores (like shoveling snow) in his place. But perhaps even tougher was the adjustment your mom and I had to make to *Mother's* absences. No, she didn't leave us. But she had to work as a housekeeper every day for some of our neighbors in order to earn extra money. Most days she worked while your mom and I were at school. But occasionally she had to leave before we did, or she returned after we had already come home from class. This meant we would have to make our own breakfast, dress ourselves, gather our books, make our lunches, and all the other stuff that's necessary just to get up and get to school. It doesn't seem hard when your mom's there. But when she isn't, you discover all that she does for you. But harder still was coming home to an empty house. A home is just a house if there's no one there to greet you after school—or so it seemed to me.

One very stormy afternoon your mom and I and a friend returned home. To our surprise, Mother was there! We didn't always walk home from school together, but this day was so bitterly cold, and the snow was blowing with such force, that I felt I should make sure your mom got home safely. I had heard stories of farmers getting lost just walking from their house to the barn. Sometimes they froze to death in those fierce Montana blizzards. So I wanted to be sure both of us made it home that day. Before Dad left us I hadn't felt as protective about your mom.

You may feel that way about Kate, Jess. It's sort of a weird thing. On one hand, she's your sister and is sometimes a pest and a pain. On the other hand, she's younger than you and sometimes needs help. Sometimes you see her as a competitor or a nuisance; at other times you see her as a friend or special person. Sometimes you want to hit her (which I hope you *never* do); at other times you want to hold her. From her point of view, she'll often see you as more than a brother. Believe it or not, she'll sometimes rely on you because she doesn't have a father close by. Scary, isn't it? It sure scared me. Mind you, the storm scared me more.

Have you ever seen or walked in a blizzard? If you haven't, let me describe what it was like. Mother woke us up that morning and rushed us through breakfast because she had to work for a neighbor all day washing and waxing floors. As we sat eating our oatmeal, the radio announcer told us that a storm was coming, with perhaps a foot of snow. Mother bundled us up as she sent us off to school, reminding us to be sure to bundle ourselves up on the way home. She left at the same time and walked off in the opposite direction. I remember looking back, and I could hardly see her, walking into the wind, just two houses away. The flat gray sky was already moaning with deep, ripping sounds as the first snow fell.

The school was only a half-mile away, but for us it seemed a long walk, especially in the gathering storm. Every step was an effort, even though the wind was behind us. It was blowing with such force that we had to hunch over as we walked to avoid being blown over. I remember seeing bits of garbage, pieces of newspaper, and even some unfortunate child's lunch bag blowing past us. When we reached the school the sky was no longer gray and moaning—it was black and howling. The snow was blowing in horizontal sheets, crashing against anything that stood in its way. As we rushed in the door, shook the snow off our parkas, and then removed them in the cloakroom, the teacher in charge had a grim look on her face. "It's going to be a big one," she said. "We may have to send you home early."

We all cheered, of course, but the teacher waved her hand, stopping us. "Rather than cheer, children," she said, "you'd better pray for those who may be stranded in the storm. I hope the Bomberdeer gets through."

About two hours later the Bomberdeer did get through. It was a hump-backed school bus on skis that picked up the schoolchildren who lived on the outlying farms. It was made by a company in Quebec called Bombardier, the same company that went on to invent snowmobiles. The Bomberdeer was a mix of tank and sled, with treads on the back and skis on the front. It looked sort of like a snowmobile on steroids. It was noisy and smoky, but it got the job done. A lot of us kids in town envied the children who got to ride in it every morning. It was a smelly, loud, adventure machine.

By the time the Bomberdeer kids had taken their places, it was almost noon. Mr. Green, the driver of the Bomberdeer, red-faced and blustering, stomped into the school and, in a loud voice that could be heard in all three classrooms, told the principal there was "no way I'm goin' out in that blast again today. Them kids are gonna hafta stay in town tonight!" Once again there was cheering, this time from the farm kids. Within an hour the principal had made the phone calls and arrangements for each student from the country to stay with a student from town. Then he sent us home.

The student assigned to us was Terry Hale, a powerfully built, red-haired farmer's son in grade three. Even though he was a year younger than I was, he was much bigger. But the biggest part of him was his smile. He was the loudest and most outgoing, most good-humored kid in the school. When the principal told us that he was coming to our house he whooped a cheer, slapped me on the back, and shouted, "Hooray! Hey, Bobby, this is gonna be a blast!"

And it *was* a blast—outside, that is. Putting on our parkas and scarves and mitts was noisy and fun. All the kids were in a holiday spirit. But when we went outside, things changed very quickly. The first problem was the door. The wind was blowing with such force that it was impossible for any of us kids to open it. Terry, who was one of the strongest, built like a human bowling ball, had some success. But even he could only open it about six to eight inches before the wind slammed it shut. Finally the principal leaned his shoulder on the door and managed to open it wide enough for us to pile out.

And pile out we did, literally! The wind had whipped all the surface snow away from the ice at the door, so that when we stepped on it our feet were blown out from under us and we were pushed into the snowbank. Your mom, Terry, two other kids, and I were piled on top of each other in a moment. We laughed and screamed with surprise and joy. This was fun! But by the time we'd gotten on our feet again the intense cold was already beginning to penetrate any chink in our armor, and our faces were starting to freeze. The principal, who helped us to our feet, told us to be careful and sent us on our way. If this were happening today, I suppose the principal would be criticized for subjecting us to the elements. But we were tougher then, and we had a frontier mentality. In those days, "when the going got tough the tough got going." So away we went.

The walk home took forever. For every step forward, it seemed the wind forced us to take two steps back. The flying snow stung our faces and coated our eyelashes with ice. Within minutes our hands and feet were numb, and all we could think of was getting out of the blizzard and into the warmth of our house. We soon discovered that the best method for walking into the wind was to form a huddle. Terry and I stood face to face, our arms around each other's shoulder, with your mom sandwiched in the middle between us. It was sort of awkward—we had to use baby steps— but it worked. Even though we could hardly see the houses lining the street, we were home in about thirty minutes. All we had to do was follow the windblown, deserted street.

When we got to our house, to our surprise Mother was waiting for us. She had come home early as well. We quickly removed our winter clothing, and within minutes we were sitting on kitchen chairs around the woodstove with our thawing feet resting on the open oven door. Mother gave each of us a mug of hot chocolate, and the warmth at our feet and in our tummies soon had us feeling very cozy and happy.

As we sat there, Mother handed me a Sears catalog that she had picked up at the post office on the way home. It was their colorful spring edition. Grabbing it from me excitedly, Terry exclaimed, "We got ours yesterday. Here, look at the bikes!" Quickly thumbing through to find the bicycle pictures, he said, "My dad is ordering *this* one for me!" And he pointed in triumph at the most beautiful bike I had ever seen.

It was red, with a tan-colored seat, whitewall tires, gleaming chrome rims and spokes, and white pinstripes on the fenders. It even had a chrome chain guard. It was awesome. It was love at first sight! I wanted that bike.

I'm going to continue this story in another letter. But before I conclude this one, I just want to add something to what I said earlier. Having no father around is tough enough. But when you add to that a mom who, because of the need for extra money, has to begin working out of the home, you may feel a bit frightened, uncertain, and insecure. You may even feel angry. Especially at times when your friends have fathers who buy them bikes.

I want you to know that hundreds of thousands of kids are going through what you're going through too. They share your hurt. There's no easy answer. But one thing is certain. If you refuse to give up, if you keep dreaming about better days ahead, if you believe, as in the fairy tales—"and everybody lived happily ever after"—you'll be a winner. And, as I found out, sometimes you do get exactly what your heart desires. Wait until you hear how I got that bike!

I love you a lot,
Uncle Bob

20

Dear Jess and Kate,

It's late at night, way past my bedtime, but I can't sleep. Aunt Jenny and I received your letters today, and I must say we're very concerned about your schoolmate, Allan, who nearly died from a drug overdose. When you said it wasn't uncommon for kids in your school to come to class high on drugs or alcohol, I was shocked! Frankly, I just didn't expect to hear that grade-schoolers were into such stuff. Drugs and alcohol can ruin your life. I'm reminded of David Hummer's story.

A few letters ago I told you about meeting the Reverend David Hummer as I was recovering from the burns I received in the fire at Slessor's barn. Do you remember how delighted I was when he told me he used to be a professional wrestler? Delight is too soft a word; *thrilled* is more like it! He had turned me off at first, asking if I'd prayed during my escape from a fiery death. But when he told me he was a wrestler, I was ready to talk with him about anything: God, the devil, or the deep-blue sea!

Before I tell you his story, there's something you've got to know. We didn't have much TV in those days, and there weren't any of today's big wrestling shows to watch on Saturdays. The only wrestlers a wrestling fan saw were *live* or pictured in a wrestling magazine. They wrestled in live matches in local arenas. They came to our town twice a year, and every time Mother bought three front-row seats. That's right. My mom, *your* grandmother, was a wrestling fan!

We knew that wrestling wasn't a legitimate competition like boxing, tennis, or any other sport, for that matter. We were aware that the wrestlers traveled together from place to place (like a circus), that they used the same dressing rooms, and that the outcome of each match was determined before they even climbed into the ring. We also knew that each match always featured a bad guy and a good guy, and the biggest name usually won. But we didn't care. The actual wrestling was real, the crowd was real, and we had a real good time booing the bad guy and cheering the good guy. It was great fun!

I remember one fight night, though, that wasn't as much fun as usual. It was held in late April during a freak spring snowstorm. Our arena was unheated. When we arrived, there were no more than two hundred fans in the seats, and it was so cold that you could see everyone's breath. When the ring announcer came out to welcome the crowd he was wearing an overcoat, a scarf, a hat, and gloves! As he introduced the first two wrestlers, they came running out in their usual wrestling shorts. But they looked unhappy (even the good guy!) and blue with cold. The cheering sounded hollow, mainly because of the thousand empty seats, and muffled, because many of us had scarves over our mouths. The wrestling itself was stiff and brief. There was the normal head-bashing outside the ring—the bad guy threw the good guy through the ropes, and he landed right in front of us. The bad guy followed, and they went at each other within arms' length of our seats. I overheard the good guy say (as the bad guy was hitting him over the head with a folding chair), "Hurry up! I'm freezin'!" There was alcohol on his breath.

David Hummer's story has a lot to do with alcohol. Here's what he told me that day at Rainbow Village.

David's mom had died when he was three years old. His father was heartbroken and vowed he'd never remarry. He spent the rest of his life as a widower and focused all of his love and attention on young David. He was a huge man, famous in their small town and the surrounding county for his strength. He was especially popular with David's young friends because he used to pick each of them up, one big hand under each of their arms, and hurl them up into the air. Many times there would be a lineup of eight or ten neighborhood kids waiting their turn to be thrown into the sky. David said that every child's reaction would be the same: chortling with nervous excitement as his dad positioned them for the launch, a scream of fear, wide-open eyes and mouths at the top of the flight, and then relieved laughing as they were caught and returned safely to the ground. "Again! Mr. Hummer, do it again" was the regular shout afterward. And he would do it again and again, to each child in turn, until he was tuckered out. He always found David to be the toughest missile to launch, mainly because he outweighed the other kids two-to-one.

He was known by the local people as "Reverend." They never called him "Mr." or "Sir." It was always "Reverend," with a mix of respect and distance in their address. He was the pastor of Zion Episcopal Church and had about forty people in his congregation. Since he was a widower, he was constantly getting pies and casseroles from female church members (especially the *single* ones!), and David got lots of mothering. In fact, David was smothered with it. The worst offender was Mrs. McWarter.

She was the church treasurer, and she kept each Sunday's offerings in a box at home. David's dad went to her place every Monday morning, and she would give him his salary for the week. Sometimes the last few dollars would be counted out in change, exactly to the penny. (Reverend Hummer found it humiliating.) Her husband was *not* a church member. He was a heavy drinker and had a wooden leg. He was also a free spirit and loved to laugh.

Mrs. McWarter took it upon herself not only to control Reverend Hummer with money, but to control David with mothering. Reverend Hummer was often called away, sometimes to visit a parishioner in the hospital in a neighboring town or to a conference or to speak at a church in another county. When he couldn't take David along, Mrs. McWarter would care for him. Reverend Hummer often wished he could have left David with others, but very few volunteered; and those who did usually offered too late. Every Monday Mrs. McWarter made sure that she knew exactly where Reverend Hummer was going to be that week. She always said, "When you're away, Pastor, leave the dear child with me. Horace (her husband) and I adore him so!" What could he do? So for that period of time, David was at her mercy.

It wasn't so bad when David was young. But as he got older, especially in grades three to five, he began to resent and even detest the woman. First she would make him take off all his clothes so she could wash them. She had a thing about cleanliness. Then she would bath him, clean his nails (ouch!), and cut his hair. After that she would cook a huge meal (mainly vegetables) and almost force-feed him, as if she were saving him from starvation. "I don't know what he feeds this boy," she'd say; "he looks absolutely a skeleton." And she'd stuff another spoonful of peas down his reluctant throat.

The worst part was bedtime. It had to be exactly on time, and it was always preceded by an hour's lecture about religion. She would sit David down on the living room sofa, pull her huge Bible off the shelf, and then pace back and forth preaching at him. David knew enough about the Bible (his dad told him great Bible stories every night) to know that Mrs. McWarter was simply using this time as a launching pad for her own ideas. Her voice would rise almost to a shriek at times, and her eyes would glisten with "holiness" as she warned him about the evils of movies, sex, women, bowling, alcohol (especially alcohol!), and anything else that she happened to see as sinful.

But the preaching that David resented most was "Remember the sabbath day to keep it holy." In her mind, this meant that on Sundays, any activity other than church attendance was evil and an offense to God. This included everything from going for a walk to playing baseball. Because David was often at her place on Sundays, he felt the full impact of this moral prison. Sunny Sundays were the worst. He'd sit in her house, a book he was supposed to be reading on his lap. When he heard the sounds of children playing outside, he'd nearly die.

The only good thing about Mrs. McWarter's house was Horace. He was everything his wife wasn't. He was quiet, thoughtful, and loved to drink. David rarely saw him without a glass of whiskey in his hand. Mrs. McWarter had tried to ban alcohol from her house years ago, but Horace always managed to stash some away somewhere. Finally she had given up. The price Horace had to pay for his sin was high—he suffered her constant nagging and condemnation. But there was one reward: she ignored him most of the day, and as long as he sat on the porch with his whiskey and cigar, he was free. He even took to eating his meals out there.

Mrs. McWarter tried to keep Horace away from David, and she succeeded by barring David from the porch. Nevertheless, she did have to go out on errands from time to time, reluctantly leaving him in Horace's care. These were times David treasured.

Horace used to sit David on his lap and talk about life. He'd ask David questions and always showed interest in and respect for his answers.

Sometimes, when David was younger, he'd let him slide down his wooden leg. One time when he was feeling especially playful, he took David outside. As he hopped around on his good leg (his *only* leg!), he pitched a ball while David batted—using Horace's wooden leg as the bat! During some of the lazy, warm days on the porch, he'd pull out a few comic books that he'd bought for David and hidden until "the wife" (as he called her) was out on some holy mission.

Horace had no use for religion and told David so. "Not that you or your father should take offense," he was quick to add. "It's just that the wife is so quick to judge and so cheerless since she got religion. She wasn't always that way, you know." And his eyes glistened with a distant memory of "the fair, lively lassie" that she once had been. As he saw it, religion took the joy out of her life.

The contrast between religion and irreligion that David saw in the McWarter household had a lasting impact on him. So did the water and whiskey Horace unwisely began giving him to drink when he entered grade five. "Time for you to grow some hair on your chest, young man," he said. One day Reverend Hummer picked his son up and, to his great displeasure, found David mildly drunk. He said nothing. But David never went to the McWarters' again. A few months later, Reverend Hummer accepted a pastorate in another town.

"What I learned later, much later, Bobby," David said to me, "was that Mr. and Mrs. McWarter were both teaching me something. Mrs. McWarter was teaching me some of the right things for the wrong reason, and Mr. McWarter was teaching me some of the wrong things for the right reason."

"Huh?" I grunted, puzzled.

"Well, it's right to be sober, chaste, and discriminating in what you do—*if* you do so for the sake of loving God and neighbor. But it's not right if you do it in order to be better or more righteous than the next guy. And it's wrong to be drunk and irresponsible because it displeases God and can even hurt your neighbor. But it's right to be free of a religion that kills your spirit. I was getting mixed messages from the McWarters. It took me thirty years to clear the confusion that resulted in my life."

"As a wrestler?" I asked.

"Yep. As a wrestler and now as a preacher."

With that he got up and said he had to make a hospital call in Mindemoya. But he promised to return and continue the story. I'll share it with you in my next letter.

Love you a lot!
Uncle Bob

21   ✍

Dear Jess and Kate,

I want to tell you more of the David Hummer story. It had such an impact on me that I never touched a drop of alcohol throughout my teenage years. Here's why.

The very first time David had a taste of Mr. McWarter's whiskey, he liked it. From that time on, he actually looked forward to going to the McWarters'. He was prepared to endure Mrs. McWarter's religious sermons and motherly clean-ups, just for those moments with Horace on the porch. The attraction was more than the whiskey; it was the combination of Horace's friendship, freedom, laughter, and the sense of "manliness" that accompanied it. The companionship he experienced on the porch was filling a real need in his life—the need to taste the bigger world outside the smaller world of the church.

What he didn't realize—*couldn't* realize at that age—was the grim fact that what appeared to him as "bigger" was actually smaller. It was a deadly trap that would lead him to a narrow little "porch" of his own. He couldn't see it then, but Mr. McWarter's porch-world was just as confining as Mrs. McWarter's church-world. It would take him years to learn that his dad was the one who really was living a balanced life and had the best of both worlds.

A few days after his first visit, David Hummer came to Rainbow Village again, this time by boat. Not just any boat, mind you, but by *tugboat!* I was now allowed to leave my bed, and that morning I was reclining on a deck chair down at the huge dock that belonged to the resort. It was made of telephone poles and railway ties. The poles formed the foundation, which contained huge rocks and boulders so that it wouldn't shift with the force of winter ice. The surface of the dock was made up of long, weathered boards that were nailed diagonally across a sub-floor of railway ties. The dock was L-shaped; the long part of the L was one hundred feet long, and the short part was fifty feet long. Uncle Bill had all the resort's boats tied to the inside of the L. I loved the sound of the waves lapping against the dock, with the boats gently tapping one another as they tugged at their lines.

As I sat in the warm morning sun reading *Tom Sawyer,* I suddenly heard the loud toot of a tugboat's whistle. It so startled me that I nearly fell out of my chair! To my complete astonishment and delight, I looked up and saw a real tugboat chugging toward the dock. It was about four hundred yards offshore, but I could see the unmistakable form of David Hummer running out onto the deck and waving at me. I waved back as enthusiastically as my burns would allow. I could hardly believe my eyes. A real tugboat! Tugboats were meant for pushing ships around in ocean harbors. What was one doing here, on Lake Kagawong, with David Hummer as captain?

To avoid breaking open my healing burns, I got up slowly and stood stiffly as David expertly edged up to the dock, jumped off to tie a front and rear line to the large rings in the poles, leaped back onto the tug to turn off the motor, and then jumped down again onto the dock with a huge grin and a, "Hi, Bobby! How's it goin'?" I answered, "Great! Where'd you get the tug?" I was still amazed at what I was seeing. It was at least fifty feet long—half the length of the big part of the dock!

"Her name's *Sarah May,* and she's seventy years old," David said proudly. "Used to be an oceangoing tug, worked several harbors down the east coast, right from New York to Carolina."

"So how'd she get here?" I asked.

"Back in the thirties there was this millionaire from Texas who had a summer home over there near Red Rock," he said, sweeping his hand toward the huge red cliffs on the far side of the lake. "He loved tugs, even though he lived in the Texas panhandle, about as land-locked as you can get. I guess he had more money than he knew what to do with. Anyway, he heard that the *Sarah May* was going to be retired, so he bought her, had her sailed to Sault

Sainte Marie, and then shipped overland to Kagawong. Just the overland part took almost two weeks and cost $200,000.00."

"Wow! How come so much?"

"Well, they had to stop and reroute traffic all along Highway 69. That took hundreds of police hours. They had to take down scores of telephone lines and put 'em back up again; several trees had to be cut to get it around corners on the island roads; and all kinds of other stuff had to be adjusted and moved. The old-timers here on the island still talk about it."

"So, is it yours now?"

"Yep. The millionaire chugged all over the lake on her for years until he died in the early forties. They drydocked her and she sat for ten years, until I bought her."

"Did she cost a lot of money?"

"Nah! They almost gave her to me. Thought I'd cut her up and sell her for scrap. But I fixed her up, and now you see her." His eyes gleamed proudly. "This is her fifth summer back on the lake."

We must have talked for an hour about *Sarah May*. I was fascinated, of course, and wanted a ride—*now!* But it was another two weeks before I had healed enough to go with David out on the lake. I'll describe *Sarah May* and tell you about my first voyage in a future letter.

Our conversation shifted. David had promised last time to continue his story. He sat beside me on the dock, and we talked until noon.

The move Reverend Hummer had made to the new church wasn't good for David. First of all, his new grade six teacher began harassing him in front of the class for being "religious," and the new church members laid guilt on him for not being religious enough. The former church had had one Mrs. McWarter; this new one had several. They made life tough for David's dad as well.

Like most ministers, Reverend Hummer wanted to keep the peace, so he spent enormous amounts of time with his congregation in their homes. Unfortunately, David was left on his own a lot, which shouldn't have been a problem (he loved to read). But, like most kids, he wanted to be accepted, so he spent equally enormous amounts of time with his schoolmates. Because of the treatment he was getting from the teacher, he acted more and more in an irreligious manner.

Since he was head and shoulders taller than his schoolmates, and because he was a born leader, he soon was "calling the tune." He overcompensated on the "religious" bit and became an out-and-out rebel—smoking, drinking, and cussin' with the best of them. With this behavior he silenced his teacher, won the acceptance of his schoolmates, and angered the Mrs. McWarters in the church. He could see Horace smiling.

By the time he reached high school he was drinking heavily. In grade ten he dropped out. A month later he left home. He was almost sixteen years old and already over six and a half feet tall.

Because of his size he had no trouble finding jobs as he worked his way toward California. He helped farmers in the harvest, worked with a roofer, and spent several weeks shoveling snow in Idaho. In many of these jobs he worked with other laborers, all of whom were older and much more road-worn. They treated him like a man, and he drank them all "under the table."

His big break came when he got a job as a bouncer at a nightclub in Los Angeles. A *bouncer,* just in case you don't know, is someone who acts as a sort of policeman and throws trouble-makers out of the club (they "bounce" on the sidewalk when they're thrown out—get it?). Well, one of the regulars at this club was a wrestler named Flapjack. He was totally bald, just as tall as David, and twice as huge. He weighed about four hundred pounds and spoke through several missing teeth with a hoarse, gravelly voice. His famous closing move in every match was to leap from the top rope down onto his opponent and squash him "as flat as a flapjack" (flapjack is another word for pancake). He was a bad guy.

Flapjack noticed David his very first night on the job. *Noticed* is too soft a word—David happened to be bouncing a very drunk patron out of the club at the very moment Flapjack was entering. David threw the drunkard out with great force (he wanted to make a good first impression). The drunken projectile happened to hit the wrestler right at the knees and sent him crashing into a line of people waiting to get into the club. You can imagine the chaos. Flapjack was like a huge bowling ball, and as he fell into that crowd they all went down like pins. Flapjack picked himself up, embarrassed. Because he had an image to maintain, he roared, "Gimme that no-good bouncer!"

He stormed into the club and came out again, with David gripped in a headlock. He made great twisting motions, as if he was pulling David's head right off. Then to David's amazement (the headlock wasn't even hurting him, by the way), as the crowd roared, Flapjack made like he was biting David's ear but was, in fact, whispering, "I'm gonna throw you to the ground and then squash you. Cooperate, and you won't get hurt!" So David cooperated, Flapjack "squashed" him with a mighty leap from the fender of a parked car, the crowd cheered, Flapjack's honor was restored, and David felt no pain (although he acted like he'd broken all his ribs). The very next day Flapjack gave David his first official lesson at a wrestling club near Malibu. In three months he was on the wrestling circuit as Flapjack's tag-team partner. They became known as "Flapjack and Billy the Kid."

Over the next several years they were the terror of the wrestling world. They became the most villainous of the bad guys and drew the biggest crowds. Sadly, they also were bad guys in real life. As they moved from town to town, from seedy motel to greasy restaurant, they drank heavily, abused women, and sometimes spent the night in jail. David would often wake up, after a night of carousing, remembering his dad and how it used to be. But that would only make his headache worse. So he'd take a drink and try to forget.

Alcohol became more important to him than food. Of course, his body began to show the effects of his work and his life-style. His wrestling skills diminished, and he started to suffer from colds, flu, and constant aches and pains. He was only twenty-five but felt sixty-five. Then Flapjack died—right in the middle of a match. He made his famous leap from the top rope, landed on his hapless opponent, and never got up.

David was devastated. Flapjack had been like a father to him. After the funeral he holed himself up in a cheap motel and had a five-day drunk.

There's more. I have yet to tell you about his short solo career in wrestling, his broken neck and near-death, and his return to his father. All that's coming soon. What a story!

We love you!
Uncle Bob

22

Dear Jess and Kate,

Have you ever heard the expression, "Sticks and stones may break my bones, but names will never hurt me"? I remember visiting a mental hospital once, and one of the patients took after me with a long list of nasty words. He called me lazy, no-good, scum, scuzz-bucket, skunk-breath, and several other even nastier names. Even though I knew the words were spoken by someone who was ill, I couldn't escape their impact (especially because I'd been feeling a bit depressed at that time).

Somehow, inside, I felt that those names were dirtying me. Worse yet, it was as though they were revealing to me that I was as unclean on the inside as I was on the outside. They were the accusers, and I was the accused. They were the judges, and I was the guilty defendant. Being called *scum* made me feel like scum. The patient was right, and I was wrong. At least, that's how I felt—after only one encounter! Imagine how children must feel after a lifetime of verbal abuse. Little wonder they sometimes act the way they do, with hatred and violence. Garbage does what garbage is.

It's easy to stand back and make wise observations and comments about abuse. We can say rightly that no child is garbage and everyone is a gift from God. We can say, again rightly, that most abusers were abused themselves as children. And we can also say that all an abused child needs is a good dose of positive affirmation to develop some healthy self-esteem. But the grim fact is that if you grow up without love you'll have a *very* difficult time accepting love in adult life. And you'll have an equally tough time showing love to someone else. Love is like a second language: if you don't learn it as a child, you may never learn it as an adult.

There is hope, however, if you're prepared to work at loving. The fact is that everyone has to choose to love, but some have a harder time choosing than others. Just as you can train your muscles to lift heavier and heavier weights through a consistent weight-training program, so you can train your heart to accept and give love. You need to take and give in small amounts, a step at a time, until one day you're as emotionally strong as someone who grew up in an atmosphere of love.

Have you ever watched gymnastics on TV? Female gymnasts are especially fascinating. All of the good ones are about your size, Kate. They look like they're about nine or ten years old, but they can do things with their bodies that are truly amazing. How come? Is it because they were born gymnasts? Nope. It's because they've received expert coaching and have spent most of their young lives in training. But never forget that they started their careers learning how to do a simple somersault. That's what abused people must do: master the simplest move first, and then grow from there. Every new move will take as much work as the first, step by step.

This reminds me of the David Hummer story. His challenge, however, was not working his way out of past parental abuse. Rather, he had to work his way out of self-inflicted abuse. After he broke his neck in the wrestling ring (talk about physical abuse!), he had to learn how to walk again—step by step.

It had been two weeks since David Hummer's last visit to Rainbow Village. On that occasion, as you remember, he had come by water on the *Sarah May*. After our visit on the dock he had sailed away, promising to return in a few weeks and take me for a ride. I looked for *Sarah May* on the lake every day after that. And every day my burns healed a bit more. They did so well that Dr. Ellison's concern switched from fire-burn to sunburn. He ordered me to keep the healing wounds protected from exposure to the sun, because the new skin was as tender as a baby's and would burn just as quickly.

I was back on the dock again, reading J. R. R. Tolkien's wonderful book, *The Hobbit.* It was six o'clock in the morning—a perfect Manitoulin morning. The sky and the lake were an identical blue, and the water was so smooth that the Red Rock cliffs on the far side appeared to be suspended between heaven and earth. As I sat at the end of the dock, it seemed that a jump into the water would be a jump into the sky. Have you ever looked at a beautiful picture and wished that you could just walk into it and become a part of it? Well, I did it that morning. I felt like I was part of a living, breathing work of art.

Remember those somersaults I was talking about a few paragraphs ago? Well, here are two of them: a love of nature and a love of books. You can learn to love both, and neither one will reject your love. Both are dangerous, mind you. Nature can be nasty, and books can be life-changing. Whether you're shooting the rapids in a death-defying canoe ride or reading an author who challenges everything you thought to be true, both will stretch your spirit. But the poetry of mountains, flowers, trees, lakes, sunrises, and sunsets can awaken within you a capacity to love that the madness of abuse would never allow. And the characters, plots, histories, and drama of books can broaden your mind when you live in the numbing shadow of an abuser. A morning on a dock with a good book opens a window for the soul.

I had been reading for about two hours when I heard *Sarah May*'s horn calling from across the lake. I looked up and could see just a little speck against Red Rock. As time went by, the speck grew until about fifteen minutes later, it was clearly the *Sarah May.* At this point she was halfway across, and she blew her horn again. I knew David had binoculars on board, so I waved. The horn blew again. David had seen me. I waved again, she blew again, and, in a few more minutes, *Sarah May* was gliding up to the dock.

She was the most beautiful tug I'd ever seen! Mind you, I'd never seen another one, but if I had, I'm sure *Sarah May* would still be the best. She had soft lines. Both bow and stern were rounded, and there was an outward swell to her sides. The bow was higher than the stern, of course, and her entire perimeter was covered in a thick rubber molding made out of sections of truck tires. Her hull and deck were made of steel and were painted in a thick red enamel. The two-story cabin was painted in a flawless white.

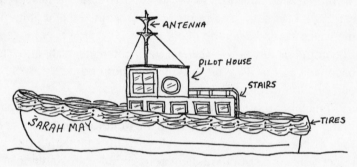

David Hummer jumped onto the dock. "Hey, Bobby! Lookin' good! How ya feelin'?"

"Great! Man, what a beauty!" I exclaimed.

"Wanna go for a ride?" he asked.

"You bet! The doctor says I can do almost anything now, except get sunburned," I said.

"Okay. So hop on!" With that, he helped me jump up onto the tug. We went into the cabin and climbed the stairs up to the pilothouse, where there was a huge oak wheel with brass ends on the spokes. David pushed the throttle ahead, and away we went. I could hardly believe it. Here I was, a boy from Montana, out on the deep blue sea in a tug. I almost pinched myself to make sure I wasn't dreaming.

Once we were offshore a few hundred yards, David let me take the wheel. Even now, as I think of it, I can feel the rush of joy that came with putting my hands on those brass spokes, pushing the throttle forward, and hearing the massive engine respond to my hand with a deep, throaty roar. I had several tons of boat and five thousand horsepower at my command. I was king of the sea!

There were several other boats out on the lake: large yachts, small fishing boats, and some water-ski boats as well. Without exception the people on these boats would smile and wave, and some would fumble around in a bag and come out with a camera to take a picture. A few times someone would beckon us, and we'd come alongside. They would carefully board *Sarah May* for a quick tour. They would be full of oohs, aahs, and admiration. They treated *Sarah May* with great respect. Because I was a part of her crew I felt that they were treating me with respect too. I liked that.

David treated every visitor with jovial friendliness and kindness. He answered each question as if it were being asked for the first time. "Where'd ya get her?" "How old is she?" "How'd it get here?" "How much horsepower?" "Where do ya dock her?" "Whaddya do with her in the winter?" "Have you ever used her for a rescue?" "I'll bet she takes a lot of fuel, huh?" "How long did it take to fix her up?" If he answered these questions once, he answered them twenty times that morning. But he was asked one question unlike all the rest by a boatload of four women.

When they pulled up beside us, I saw that all four were in their late twenties or early thirties, and they were all wearing bikinis. Bikinis were just coming into fashion in those days, and many people considered them scandalous.

They made some of the usual comments about *Sarah May*, but I could see their interest was more in David than in nautical knowledge. They seemed to hover around him and giggle a lot. As they were leaving one woman said, "We're having a party at our cottage tonight; would you like to come?" Without hesitating David answered, "Thanks, but I've got a meeting at the church."

"Oh, I'm sorry. It's gonna be a great time!" She looked him up and down slowly and said, "Maybe another time." With a fetching smile she disembarked and drove off.

"Who're they?" I asked, still impressed with the display of tanned flesh.

"Oh, those women are divorcees who live to party, and unfortunately, many of their parties have caused real heartache in some of the marriages around here."

I didn't need to ask any more questions. I knew exactly what he meant. David took the wheel. As we took off, he said, "Bobby, there's always gonna be women who want a good time—and you'll be tempted to accept their offers. God knows I did, especially in my wrestling years. But I've learned something: if you show no respect for women, even immodest women, in a strange sort of way you show no respect for yourself. Always choose to do what's right, and you'll gain a great reward: self-respect."

"Yeah, but how do you avoid doing things you don't want to do and still not hurt the women's feelings?" I asked.

"Treat 'em like sisters," David answered. "Treat 'em like sisters."

That's some of the best advice David, or anyone for that matter, ever gave me. It had real power, because I saw that David practiced what he preached. His example became one of those somersaults I talked about earlier. The respect of others, combined with self-respect, gives tremendous strength.

Well, it's time to wrap this up. I'm so happy you're enjoying my letters. I'm certainly enjoying yours!

I'll write again next week.

Love you,
Uncle Bob

P.S. In the next letter, I'll tell you about the rest of David's wrestling career. Promise!

23 _____ ✍

Dear Jess and Kate,

I'll never forget something David Hummer said to me as we rode around the lake that day on the *Sarah May*. I think he was reflecting on what he'd just said to me about the Mrs. Burdens of the world. He slowed *Sarah May* right down and shut off the motor. As we sat in the middle of the lake, drifting, he looked me straight in the eye and said, "Ya know, Bobby, my dad once said that we are all monuments to the decisions we've made. I believe it. I've proven it in my own life."

"Tell me about it," I said, thrilled that I was about to hear more of his story. We took two chairs down to the deck and sat down. David tilted back in his chair and began.

"After Flapjack died I had to make a decision. Would I continue wrestling? And if I did, would it be with another partner in a tag-team, or would it be solo? I talked to my agent about it, and he recommended that I go on my own. He figured the fans would sympathize with my loss of Flapjack. I could play on that sympathy and thereby become a good guy. Sure enough, he was right. The fans started cheering rather than booing me, and I became very popular. In fact, the organizers of our wrestling federation began to develop a strategy that would result in my becoming world champion. I was really on a roll.

"I was making more money, sleeping with more women, and drinking more than ever before. Other wrestlers envied me. I was at the top of my game, and I felt more miserable than I ever had in all my life."

"Why?" I asked. "How come you were so miserable?"

"Well," David's brow wrinkled in thought, "let me put it this way. When you're poor and miserable, you think that money will bring happiness. When you're sick and miserable, you think that health will bring you happiness. When you're unknown and miserable, you think that popularity will bring you happiness. When you're sexually frustrated and miserable, you think that sex will bring you happiness. Imagine your shock, then, when you get all you want—money, health, popularity, sex—and you discover that your misery had nothing to do with the lack of things at all, because you're still miserable. Misery, like happiness, has no regard for what you have or don't have. Rather, it has everything to do with what you are. I was selfish and immature. My god, and my devil, was my pleasure. I could satisfy my needs for the moment with a bottle or a woman, but I could only dull the heartache. I had chosen a life of diminishing returns."

"Diminishing returns?" I asked. "I don't understand."

"It's like this. Suppose your life is a savings account in the bank. Every time you want to please yourself, you make a withdrawal. For a while, your every want is satisfied. But eventually your savings are depleted, and there's nothing more to withdraw. You're broke because you didn't deposit anything.

"The only way to make a deposit is to seek the good of others. If you commit yourself to doing that, your resources never run dry. And the funny thing about doing good is that the more you do it, the less you're attracted by selfish behavior. Doing good, doing what's right, is a reward in itself."

"So the more you drank, the more you spent, the more you slept with women, the less you enjoyed it?" I asked.

"Exactly! I think this is why people who spend all their lives pursuing pleasure end up as bitter, cynical old people. They feel wasted, because they *are* wasted. Life is not meant for self-absorption. It's meant for giving. But all I did was take. Thank God I broke my neck."

"What? Thank God for a broken neck? You gotta be kidding," I exclaimed.

"No. I'm serious. I was in a match with one of the top bad guys, Beauteous Brutus, when—"

"Beauteous Brutus?" I cut him off. I couldn't believe it. He was one of the most famous villains in wrestling history.

"Yep. Beauteous Brutus. And the plan was for us to fight to a draw. We were supposed to end the match with both of us lying exhausted on the mat. That way the ref wouldn't be able to declare a winner. This would set us up for a big semifinal match a few months later. We had rehearsed a move where he picked me up in a bear hug from behind, then threw me over the top rope. I would land on my back; he would leap over the ropes to administer the coup-de-grace by landing on my chest; and I would roll out of the way at the last minute. He would fall on the floor, and then we would fight it out with chairs that happened to be leaning against the ring. Those chairs were specially designed to fall apart when we hit each other with them. They were real crowd-pleasers.

"We had done this act in several arenas, and every time the crowd yelled for more. But one hot night, in an overcrowded arena in Mississippi, something went terribly wrong. Beauteous Brutus picked me up in the bear hug all right, but as he threw me over the ropes my foot caught in the top rope. Instead of falling on my back, I fell on my head. When Beauteous Brutus came flying down on me, I couldn't move out of the way as planned, and he landed full force on my chest. When I woke up about five minutes later, I knew I'd been seriously injured."

"Did you know your neck was broken?"

"I wasn't sure. But I had this strange sense of distance from my body. I could see my arms and legs, but I couldn't feel them. Beauteous Brutus knew right away. His face was white with concern.

"Of course, the crowd thought it was all part of the show. They cheered and booed lustily as I was carried out on a stretcher and Brutus was declared the winner. I was rushed to the hospital, and William—Brutus' real name was William Horton—stayed the whole night at my bedside. They had me so full of painkillers that I was barely conscious. But I did hear William praying for me.

"The next morning the doctors came in and performed several tests. They kept me totally immobile and wouldn't let me move, even to go to the bathroom."

"So how did you do it?" I asked.

"You don't want to know," David groaned. "At about four o'clock that afternoon one of the doctors came back in and told me the news. He said I'd broken my neck, and there was very little chance that I'd ever recover control of my body from the chest down. He said I'd be able to partially use my arms, but I should expect to be in a wheelchair for the rest of my life."

"How'd you take it?"

"Not too well. That's when I prayed. It was the first time I could remember praying since I was a kid in Sunday school."

"What did you pray?"

"Basically, 'Please God, help me!' I also tried to make deals, like, 'If you heal me I'll donate all my money to charity.' Or 'Heal me and I'll never drink again.' Stuff like that."

"I don't believe in God," I said a bit too quickly.

"To be frank, I don't think I did either," David answered. "Well, I did, but I didn't. I believed way down deep in my heart, but I lived like I didn't believe. I guess that when it came to God, I lived in denial."

"Huh?"

"Denial. Like when you've got a paper to write, but it's such a beautiful Saturday that you go out and play all day instead of studying. For the day, at least, you live as though there were no paper and no future day of reckoning. When the day arrives to turn in your paper, however, you experience a sudden jolt of reality. Denial gives way to sheer panic. Has that ever happened to you?" he asked.

"Yep. More than once," I admitted.

"Me too. I lived as though I was accountable to no one, as if all that mattered was getting what I wanted. But the broken neck changed all that."

"How?"

"First of all, I couldn't deny that my first reflex, when told I would never walk again, was to ask God for help. Secondly, I had a lot of time—a *lot* of time—flat on my back, to think."

"What did you think about?"

"Oh, all kinds of stuff. The error of my ways, my childhood, friends, enemies, Dad—I thought a lot about him. And I spent a lot of time talking with him. As soon as he heard about my accident, he drove down to Mississippi and stayed for a month. We talked every day.

"You know what amazed me about my dad? Not once in all that talking did he ever condemn me for the choices I had made. Not once! It was as though I'd never made a bad decision in my life."

"Maybe he was living in denial," I chuckled weakly.

"Nope. It wasn't denial. It was compassion. Love. This hit me like a ton of bricks. You see, I'd been away from home since I was a teenager. So when I thought of Dad, I saw him as that big authority figure he had been in my childhood. I had never thought of him as a person with needs. I hadn't thought about the pain of his loneliness, his ongoing grieving for Mother, the burdens of pastoring a bunch of Mrs. McWarters. I didn't see his fears, his hurts, his insecurities. Rather, I saw him as a hindrance to my desire for independence. It wasn't until I met him man to man, in that hospital room, over all those hours, that I realized the depth of his love for me. And that realization awoke a love for him that had barely been alive all those years, way down deep in my heart. He had always been my dad—but over those weeks he became my father."

"Huh? What do you mean by that?" I asked, puzzled.

"I mean, when I was a kid he had just been there, outside of my life, somehow. Now he was in here, in my heart, inside my very being. He became the very best friend I had ever known. Before, I acknowledged him; after, I *loved* him. And I still do."

I was amazed to see tears in David's eyes. And I was envious too. I wished I could feel about my dad the way he felt about his. We just sat and looked at the water for about ten minutes. There didn't seem to be much more to say. And I was happy to suspend any talk about God. I was sort of enjoying being an atheist.

Well, there certainly is much more to tell. And, as I always do, I promise to continue the story soon. Please write me. I really love your letters. So does Aunt Jenny!

Love to you and your mom,
Uncle Bob

24   ✍

Dear Jess and Kate,

Boy, I sure was surprised to hear that you had already seen a tugboat! I had forgotten about your trip to Baltimore last summer. The tug you saw was probably one used on the Atlantic Intracoastal Waterway. I understand that it runs from Boston all the way to Key West. That's twelve hundred miles! Wouldn't it be fun to ride a boat the whole way? I think it takes about ten days for a one-way run. I wonder if the *Sarah May* ever worked those waters? I'll have to call David Hummer and find out. David is seventy now, and he's as healthy and vigorous as if he were forty. And his father is still alive! He's ninety and still chops wood every day! They live together in a cottage on Lake Mindemoya, and they've got a woodpile that's two hundred feet long and six feet high. Old Reverend Hummer has chopped enough wood for every fireplace on the island! He's an outstanding person. Let me tell you some of his story.

Howard Hummer was born in the early 1900s on a farm near International Falls, Minnesota. He was eleven pounds at birth, and everyone expected he'd grow up to be as big as his father. When his father saw him a few hours after his birth, he felt Howard's chest and shoulders and declared, "He's a big one, all right. He's gonna be a 'solid Jackson.'" There were no Jacksons in the family; it was just an expression used by all the Hummers (including Howard and David) to describe someone really strong. I remember one day, when I was helping Uncle Bill lift a boat out of the water at Rainbow Village, David came along and helped us. When we were finished, and I was puffing with the effort, David slapped me on the shoulder and said, "Good job, Bobby. You lifted a lot of weight there. You keep doing that and one day you'll grow up to be a real solid Jackson." He then squeezed my upper arm and observed, "Hard fat like a hen's face," which was another expression handed down from his father. And, wouldn't you know it, I use the same expressions even now.

Howard was born into a very healthy, happy family. His mom and dad loved each other and showed it. As he grew up, it seemed he was always seeing his dad hugging his mother, telling her how beautiful she was and how much he loved her. His older brother and younger sister were also very loving to each other, to him, and to their parents. As you might expect, there was a lot of laughter in the Hummer household. It was a home with a strong heart.

Then, one stormy winter Sunday, disaster struck. Howard's family had gone into town to attend church. They had considered staying home because of the storm. But Howard's dad was one of those guys who takes bad weather as a personal challenge; he hated to give in to "just a little snow." So they had gone. Howard stayed at home with his grandmother because he had a cold. When his family failed to return at noon, Howard and his grandma weren't too concerned. In fact, they expected them to be late. But as the afternoon wore on without their return, Howard's grandma started making some phone calls. She called the pastor, who said that, yes, the Hummers had been at church that morning. She called the police and was told that they had a backlog of fender-benders to attend to, but no, they had no report of an accident involving the Hummers. And she called the neighbors, but drew a blank there as well. Then the phone lines went dead. Somewhere along the line, the heavy snow had broken or fouled up the wires.

It wasn't until the next morning that they got the news. Howard looked out his bedroom window and saw a solitary figure on a horse, plodding through the blowing snow. He dressed quickly and ran down to the kitchen, just as he heard the knock at the door. He opened it, and there stood Pastor Shultz, covered in snow, with a sad look in his eyes. Howard invited him in. After he hung up the pastor's coat, Howard ran upstairs to get Grandma. She had just dressed and was on her way down, a look of concern on her face.

"Is that someone at the door?" she asked.

"Yes. It's Pastor Shultz. He came on horseback," Howard answered.

"Oh dear! I wonder what's happened?" she half whispered, more to herself than to Howard.

It didn't take long for Pastor Shultz to tell the story. Howard's family had left the church in their Model T Ford. They had managed to go about a mile in the driving blizzard, but had gotten stuck right on the railway tracks on the outskirts of town. Before they could get off the tracks, the train had struck. It hadn't even stopped. The engineers hadn't seen the Model T; nor had they felt it. Howard's family were all killed, and they weren't discovered until late that night, when Fred Bulman, the town's blacksmith, came by in his horse-drawn sled.

How does one describe grief? Especially the kind that follows a sudden bereavement. In many ways, I think it's like any other unexpected trauma, yet a hundred times worse.

For example, I remember breaking my ankle playing basketball in high school. I went up for a rebound and landed with my right foot on top of another player's foot. My ankle twisted and broke with a crunching snap. I fell in a heap on the floor, writhing in agony. For a moment it was as though I could see nothing, hear nothing, but only feel the electric jabs of pain shooting from my ankle to every part of my body. Very quickly, though, as my teammates gathered around, the intensity of the pain gave way to a dull, deep ache. As I was taken to the hospital, my ankle was pleasantly numb, and I was almost jovial as I described the injury to the driver.

But when I was asked to wait in the emergency room, then wheeled to the X-ray department, and wheeled back to a bone-setting room, the narcotic effects of shock began to wear off. Every movement hurt. And when the doctor began to probe my ankle with his fingers, and then set it, it was as though he were breaking it all over again. It was awful. That night as I lay in bed, with my leg in a cast, I hardly slept. The pain was nearly killing me. It turned out that the cast was too tight, so the next day the doctor had to cut it off and start all over again. Another sleepless night followed. But over time the pain subsided, and three weeks later the cast was removed for good. It took months, however, to regain the ankle's strength. To this day, I have to tape it whenever I want to play tennis or shoot a few baskets. It will never be quite the same again.

When Howard Hummer heard that his father, mother, brother, and sister were all dead, the pain was worse than if he had broken both arms and both legs. Much worse. He felt as if he'd just been stabbed with a hot knife in the stomach. A knot of agony suddenly gripped his heart, and he felt that his very life was being violently squeezed from him. The blood drained from his face, his eyes rolled back in their sockets, his knees buckled, and he slumped to the floor, unconscious.

He regained consciousness in his grandmother's arms, his head to her sobbing breast. Pastor Shultz was praying, and the snow was beating on the windows.

After a few minutes Pastor Shultz, seeing that he was alert, said, "Howard, we're going to have to go into town. Do you think you could harness the horse to the sleigh? We've got to go now, or I fear we may be stranded here by the blizzard."

"Sure, Pastor," he said numbly. As he put on his parka and boots, he felt like he was walking in a bad dream.

He went out to the barn, got old Nellie out of her stall, and harnessed her up to the sleigh. It was a beautiful "one-horse open sleigh" like the one we sing about in the Christmas song "Jingle Bells." Every winter in his memory, Howard had gone for rides with his family in that sleigh. Just a week ago they had done so, and he could hear his mom in her girlish soprano voice leading them,

> Jingle bells! Jingle bells!
> Jingle all the way.
> Oh what fun it is to ride,
> In a one-horse open sleigh!

He sat on the edge of the sleigh and wept. Pastor Shultz found him sitting there ten minutes later. He was in a daze. His eyes and nose were running, and the snow was sticking to his face.

"Good job, Howard," the pastor said gently. "Do you think you could drive the sleigh over closer to the door? It would save your grandma from having to walk too far in all this snow."

"Sure. Sure thing, Pastor," Howard replied. His voice sounded distant and muffled to his own ears. He felt like he was watching himself as he slid into the seat and slapped the reins on Nellie's back. His body was going through the motions, but his spirit was bruised and broken.

The next few days were a blur. He and his grandmother stayed with the Shultzes, and there were endless visitors, words of sympathy, and cups of tea. He was sleeping in an unfamiliar bed, eating unfamiliar food, and living with unfamiliar people. All he wanted was to go home, to eat his mom's cooking, to hear his little sister's piping voice, and to laugh with his father and brother again. He felt so alone.

The funeral was brief and sad. When they got out to the cemetery, snow started to fall. Four graves had been chopped out of the frost-hardened ground by two shifts of hard-working diggers. The pine coffins were lowered into the ground; some artificial grass was placed on top of them; and everyone hurried away in the developing storm. Howard was taken back to the Shultzes' home, where many of the mourners had come for refreshments. He was hugged, patted, and generally fussed over until he felt that he had to escape. He was given all kinds of advice, offers of help, and condescending comments such as, "There's a good boy." "Brave little lad." "Oh, poor wee man." "My! My! Such a load for a youngster." "Sad little orphan." And on and on. All he wanted was his father's hand on his shoulder and his mother's voice in his ear.

Later that evening the shock began to wear off, and Howard had his worst night yet. His heart had been broken. But now the sharp pulses of pain gave way to a dull, throbbing ache. Memory after memory flashed by, and every one only added to the depth of the fracture. The memories brought no comfort. He cried until he could cry no more. Then, limp and wasted, he fell into a black sleep.

Weeks would pass before he could get through a day without sorrow. And it took the rest of his life to come to grips with the wound he had suffered.

You know, sometimes divorce can be like a death. In some ways it may be even worse, because the person who has "died" is still alive. It's sort of like a living death.

I'll bet there have been times (and still are) when you've felt that way about your parents' divorce. You have grieved and felt like your heart was broken. I want you to know something: just like a broken ankle, your injury will heal. But things will never again be quite the same. From time to time, now and in the future, you'll have moments of real pain. Sometimes you'll feel anger, regret, or guilt. But without question, you'll have to "tape that ankle." When you decide to commit your heart to someone in marriage, you'll wonder if divorce might happen to you too. It's only natural to think that way.

But there's something about broken bones I haven't mentioned yet. If the doctor sets it right, and it heals well, the *join* (as it's called) will be stronger than the original bone. It will never break in that spot again.

So be encouraged. When a broken heart heals, it becomes stronger than before the break. Just give it time.

Speaking of time—it's time to go! I'll write again next Thursday.

Love ya,
Uncle Bob

25_____

Dear Jess and Kate,

Today my thoughts are on being poor. In another letter I talked about how there seems to be less money after a divorce and how moms usually have to work outside the home. It's tough. But it can be a lot less tough. In fact, you *can* be poor and happy. It all depends on your attitude. What do I mean by *attitude*? Let me tell you about Roddy Thornton.

Roddy was my age and lived in the biggest house in town. His father owned several businesses; the best known was Thornton's Hardware Store. Roddy was an only child and got everything he wanted. I've never forgotten the first time I saw his playroom.

It was a sunny Sunday afternoon in June, and a bunch of us kids were playing baseball at the school grounds of Ben Franklin High. The game had been going on for some time, and many of the players had dropped out and gone home. Finally, just a handful of us were left. We were all getting a bit bored when Alan Burton piped up, "Hey, guys! Let's go slide the chute!" We all shouted our agreement: "Yes! Let's do it!" and ran around to the far side of the school building.

The chute was a huge tubular fire escape that rose at a 60-degree angle (steep!) from the ground all the way up to the top floor of the school building. It was about four feet in diameter and was made of smooth steel. The tube ran parallel to the ground for about ten feet before it began its fearsome ascent. I found it both scary and irresistible. I had my shoes and socks off in a flash.

We had to have bare feet to get traction when climbing up inside the chute. In fact, we needed both feet and both hands. We'd climb, bent over on all fours, seeking a grip on the smooth surface. It was very tiring. Sometimes we'd straighten our legs and push our backs against the top of the chute just to rest. (That's why we sometimes pulled our shirts up to our shoulders—our bare backs had more of a grip on the slippery tube than our shirts did.) As you'd expect, sometimes one of us near the top would lose traction, slip, and slide at a ferocious speed to the bottom, knocking everyone further down in the tube off their feet. We'd land in a heap at the bottom, laughing and wrestling, eager to climb in and try again.

As I said, it was scary—not just because of the height, but because of the darkness. The closer we got to the top, the darker it got. The only source of light was the opening at the bottom.

When resting (with your feet, hands, and back all pushing against the sides), if you looked between your legs, back to the bottom, you would see the light reflecting with decreasing brightness all the way to your bare feet. It was like being in the barrel of a cannon.

So the closer we got to the top, the darker and the slipperier it got. Right at the top, the tube cut at a sharp angle into a small circular door in the wall of the school, providing a three-foot ledge where we could sit and catch our breath before the death-defying slide to the bottom. Sometimes three or four of us would scrunch up on that ledge, hook our legs around each other, and hurtle down like a human train. At other times we'd leave at two-second intervals, and the game was to hit the ground and roll out of the way before the next guy crashed into you. And, of course, we would often go solo, screaming and yelling all the way. It was wonderful fun!

One of the kids who came to slide the chute with us that day was Roddy Thornton. He didn't play with us that much. He liked playing, but I think his mother saw most of us kids as "beneath" her son. Nothing was too good for him. She kept him well fed (so well he was very overweight), bought him any toy he wanted (more about that in a minute), and made sure he played with no one but those of equal wealth (which meant he played alone). He was a spoiled rich kid. And, as I was about to find out, he was miserable.

We'd been sliding the chute for about an hour when Roddy joined us. He didn't say anything, but simply climbed in behind four of us as we started up the huge incline. As we grunted our way to the top, Mickey Salton, who was in the lead, yelled back, "Hey, Roddy! How come you're here?"

"My parents are away," came the reply, his voice sounding tinny and hollow in the tube. "I've got a sitter this weekend." Nothing more was said, and we kept climbing. We were almost at the top when Mickey slipped. With a yell he crashed into me; then we crashed into the next guy, and the next. Finally we hit Roddy at the knees and slid with a frightening speed to the bottom, exploding in a tangle of legs and arms out of the chute and onto the ground with a thud. Unfortunately for Roddy, most of the thud was his body hitting the ground, with the rest of us on top of him. We quickly sprang to our feet, laughing and shouting, ready for more, when we saw Roddy lying face down, barely moving. We rolled him over on his back, but he just lay there, his eyes bugging out and his mouth moving wordlessly. There was panic on his face.

"Quick! Pump his legs!" Mickey shouted, instantly recognizing Roddy's condition. "He's had his wind knocked out."

Rainer Rourke and I each grabbed a leg and started pushing Roddy's knees down onto his chest in a pumping motion, while Mickey and the others shouted encouragement. For a moment I thought Roddy had a more serious problem, because his face started to grow deathly white and his eyes began to roll back into his head. But in about ten seconds we heard a high wheezing sound that turned into a thin scream. It was Roddy. The color had returned to his face, and now his eyes were filling with tears. His chest started to heave. With a look that seemed more of embarrassment than pain, he kicked Rainer and me away, stumbled to his feet, and ran away, wailing. We all started to laugh, but as he staggered toward the school's gate, I suddenly felt sorry for him. He was a pathetic sight. Even though none of us liked him, I felt that maybe I should make sure he got home safely. So, without a word, I took off after him.

"Hey! Where are you goin'?" I heard Mickey exclaim as I sprang away.

"You're not worried about that crybaby, are ya?" But I didn't turn to answer. When I caught up with Roddy at the street, I looked back. Mickey and the boys had already disappeared into the chute.

Roddy, who had stopped running by now, heard me behind him and turned around. His face wet with tears and his voice thick with emotion, he blurted out, "Go away, kid. I don't need no help." He tried to run away, tripped, and fell flat. As I helped him to his feet, he shook me off, shouting, "I said go away! Don't you understand English?"

I backed off, a bit startled, and said, "Okay. I just wanted to make sure you were all right."

"Sure. I'll bet you just wanted another laugh," he said bitterly, and walked away. Feeling a little puzzled, I began walking home. I'd gone about a hundred yards when I heard Roddy's voice calling, "Hey, kid! Wanna play with my toys?"

I turned, and there he was, standing just about where we'd parted, his hands shoved in his jeans pockets. It took only a moment to answer, "Sure!" And I ran to catch up to him. I'd heard about Roddy Thornton's fabled playroom, but no one I knew had ever been there. Who knows? Maybe I'd be the first kid in town to see it.

We didn't talk much as we walked to his house. Of course, I asked him how he was, and he said he was okay. He kept calling me kid, so I told him my name and was surprised to learn that he knew the names of only a handful of the children in town. It didn't take long for me to determine that Roddy had no friends. "They're all just a bunch of jerks anyway," he said, referring to the kids at school. (I guess it didn't occur to him that this sweeping description included me.) I remember wondering, as we reached his front door, if maybe I was making a mistake. Who would want to play with a guy who figured the whole town was beneath him?

From the outside, Roddy's house reminded me of a picture of Fort Knox I'd seen in a book. It was a huge, flat-faced, white cement structure that looked more like a bank than a house. As we walked in I half expected to see tellers, long counters, and security guards. Instead, we were met by a gleaming white marble floor, ceramic dogs guarding a massive oak staircase, and a bored baby-sitter, sitting on the stairs doing her nails. She didn't even look up as Roddy led me upstairs to his playroom.

The playroom was like Sears' Christmas catalog come to life. It was a large, bright, black-and-white tiled room full of toys. I mean *full*. There were racing cars, power shovels, bulldozers, dump trucks, motorcycles, fire engines, tanks, airplanes, toy soldiers, army jeeps, and—wonder of wonders—an electric train that ran around the entire room on a raised platform. I looked at all this and gasped so loudly that Roddy asked me if something was wrong. "Wrong? With me?"

I replied, "No, not a thing. I'm just amazed at all these toys! It must be wonderful to have all this!"

"S'pose so." Roddy answered, with a total lack of enthusiasm. "Actually, I'm kinda bored with this stuff."

"Bored?" I couldn't believe my ears. "How can you be bored? You've got everything a kid could want!"

"Nope. Not everything. What I really want is a new fire engine."

"A new fire—" I stopped in midsentence, staring directly at three beautiful red fire engines sitting on the floor.

"Oh, those are nuthin'," Roddy said, following my stare. "You should see the one I saw in a toy store last month in New York!" He then went on to describe a radical, battery-powered toy (battery power was new in those days) that actually shot real water through its hoses and raised and lowered its ladders at the push of a switch. "Man! I'd give anything for that," he said, "but Dad said I'd have to wait until next time he travels to New York. I don't want to wait. I want it *now!*" he said, with a pout and a greedy look in his eye. I was speechless. How could a kid be blind to all he had just because of something he didn't have? Finally I mumbled, "Let's play with the bulldozers." And we played for about two hours with the bulldozers and pretty well everything else. But to my surprise, it wasn't as much fun as I thought it would be. The lack of the battery-powered fire engine seemed to have taken the edge off the fun. In fact, I clearly remember thinking that I regularly had more fun playing with homemade and secondhand toys. In Roddy Thornton I had run into a kind of poverty I'd never known existed.

Mine was a poverty of little. My toys were few and well used, and I didn't even have a bicycle. His was a poverty of much. He had *so* much, in fact, that the only joy a toy held for him was the joy of wishing he had it, the joy of fantasizing, hoping, dreaming. But as soon as he got it, it lost its luster and became just another part of the clutter. I know this is true, because the next time I was at his place, the recently acquired battery-operated fire engine was on its side in a corner, neglected and forgotten. Roddy was dreaming about a new racing car now. An attitude of gratitude was beyond him. He didn't think in terms of being thankful; he thought only in terms of wanting more.

Roddy Thornton taught me something else about poverty. Even though he had both parents living at home, he rarely spent time with them. His dad was always in a meeting or away on business, and his mom treated him more like a boarder than a son. To show their love they gave him things rather than themselves. Roddy was starving in the middle of all that wealth; he literally had no one who loved him. In every sense of the word he was a poor little rich boy.

Jess and Kate, I've said it before and I'm sure I'll say it again: You are rich because you are loved. You may feel sometimes that your dad doesn't love you because he left, but I'm sure he *does* love you. Your mom loves you. Aunt Jenny and I love you. Sure, sometimes you'll wish you had more things than you do. But when you do, try to remember Roddy Thornton. In all my life I don't think I've ever met anyone poorer.

Love ya,
Uncle Bob

26

Dear Jess and Kate,

Shalom! You won't believe where I'm writing from. I'm sitting on our hotel room balcony looking across the Kidron Valley to the Old City of Jerusalem! I didn't tell you that Aunt Jenny won a trip to Israel because I wanted to surprise you. We're thrilled because we couldn't have afforded it otherwise. We've been here three days already, and we just love it. Our hotel is small, cheap, and a bit scuzzy, but the view is stunning! I was wide awake at 4:30 this morning (couldn't sleep—jet lag!), so I got dressed quietly (Aunt Jenny was sawing logs!) and went out for a *five-*hour walk. Let me tell you about it.

First of all, I'll draw you a rough map of the Old City so you can follow me as I walk. I've traced my route with a dotted line.

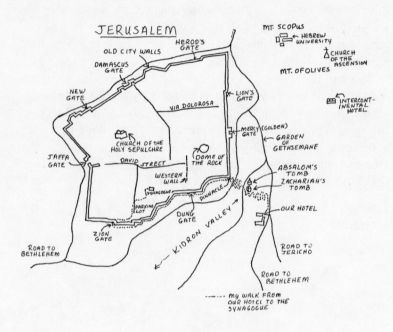

The best way I can describe my impressions, as I walked out into Jerusalem's early dawn, is peace and quiet. Many times over the years I've heard people (parents, teachers, Aunt Jenny, etc.) say, "All I want is some peace and quiet." Usually they say it with a measure of resentment in their voice, as if someone, or just the general atmosphere, has robbed them of a personal possession. I've done it myself. Well, let me tell you something. I've never known peace and quiet such as I experienced this morning. It's almost something physical. You hear it. You smell it. You touch it. You walk through it, as though you were parting a thick, unseen mist. It makes you want to breathe as deeply as possible, as though you could take it into your very soul. You want to sing, but without making any sound. Your heart swells with the joy of a silent symphony as you walk along. It's a living peace and a breathing quiet. I almost walked on tip-toe, so as not to break the spell.

The first thing I saw across the valley and slightly below me as I walked out of the hotel was the Old City of Jerusalem, still asleep in the twilight of early dawn. The ancient stone walls were a faint purple, and the golden dome of the huge mosque dominating the eastern view of the city glowed with a faint luster in the soft morning light.

Immediately across the valley from where I stood was the southeast corner of the wall, rising majestically into the air. (I read in a guidebook that it is called "the pinnacle of the temple.") Between me and the pinnacle was the very steep, V-shaped valley called *Kidron*. When I say V-shaped, I mean it. From where I was standing, the bottom of the valley looked no more than fifty feet across, while the sides must have sharply descended at least two hundred feet! The distance from the pinnacle to the northeastern corner of the wall seemed to be about half a mile. The distance from the pinnacle to the southwestern corner looked to be about the same. This meant that I could see almost the entire city from where I stood.

Inside the walls I could see a tangle of domed roofs, delicate towers (called *minarets*), church steeples, mosques, construction cranes, and television antennas. The tangle seemed to dip about halfway between the eastern and western walls and rise a bit toward the west, making the western side of the city seem higher than the eastern side. Then, as I was taking all this in, the city changed before my very eyes. Almost imperceptibly the purple tint of the walls changed to a violet color. Then, about three or four minutes later, the violet gave way to a light pink. In another few minutes the pink became rose. Then the rose gave way to a faint yellowish-white. The sun was rising behind the Mount of Olives, and Jerusalem was about to get its wake-up call.

Right on cue I heard the loud cry of a rooster from somewhere down in the village that grew up the eastern slope of the Kidron

Valley. He crowed lustily for about a minute. Then I heard the harsh hee-hawing of a donkey coming from roughly the same direction, below me to the south. After that, a *very* loud voice started to chant from one of those minarets in the Old City. It was the Muslim call to prayer, and it must have gone on for at least five minutes. Suddenly I saw movement—a man riding a donkey in the valley, a woman carrying a basket on her head by the pinnacle, an empty bus dieseling up the hill toward me from the direction of the Garden of Gethsemane, and a dog chasing a cat on the road behind me. Jerusalem was stretching her arms and wiping sleep from her eyes. Another Sabbath had begun.

You can see on the map that our hotel is located on the slope of the Mount of Olives. What you can't see is how steep that slope is. As I walked along the road toward the Garden of Gethsemane, I decided to cut down and through the old graveyard all the way to the bottom of the valley. At some points my feet were slipping and sliding on the slope. At one point particularly, I almost had a serious fall. That point was a sudden opening that came upon me without warning. It was a huge, three-sided hole, cut into the side of the hill. In the middle of it, beneath me, was an ancient pyramidlike structure chiseled out of rock. I gingerly walked around the hole, then slid, more than stepped, fifty feet down to the valley floor for a closer look.

As I stood there looking *up* at the structure, I was surprised to see that there was another one, of a different shape entirely, cut out of the rock about sixty or seventy feet to the left. All around them were smaller holes and caves, some of which were bordered with carved stone. Both structures were about forty or fifty feet high, having square walls with pillars carved into them and carved stairs at the base. The roof of the first one, as I've already said, looked like a stone pyramid, and the other one had a round roof with what looked like an inverted birdbath on the top. I was wondering how these things had been cut right out of the base of the mountain when I suddenly heard a bleating sound. I looked behind me, and there was a flock of about one hundred sheep coming up the valley.

They were a remarkable sight, mainly because of their color, which was the same as the surrounding limestone. Usually when you think of sheep, you think of white woolly creatures, like balls of cotton, grazing in green pastures. Not here. I've noticed that everything has a sunburned, dusty hue—including the sheep! They blend so well into the landscape that they almost appear to be woolly stones moving along the ground.

The sheep walked past me and around me, as if I were a stone myself. They took no notice of me as they nosed here and there, with their chocolate-brown faces, looking for tufts of grass or clumps of weeds. Close at hand, I saw that they were dirty, dusty, and *very* smelly (they had nobody telling them every night to take a bath, Jess!). Their wool was scraggly and heavily matted, and they had long, floppy brown ears and trusting brown eyes. "But where's the shepherd?" I asked myself.

To my surprise, the shepherd was following rather than leading. In a moment or two I saw him about one hundred yards down the valley, walking slowly behind the last few stragglers. Whenever a sheep veered off on its own or took too long with a tuft of grass, he would throw a stone at the sheep and shout a command. As he got closer I saw that he was carrying a small walking stick, which he sometimes used to swat a reluctant sheep. He was dressed in a baggy pair of pants and a tattered Toronto Blue Jays shirt and was barefoot. He was no more than twelve years old.

I waved at him as he approached, and he flashed a huge, white-toothed smile. Their whiteness stood out in the dusty atmosphere and looked all the whiter because of his sunburned skin. He reached into his pocket as he came up to me and pulled out some old coins, which he held out in his open palm.

"American?" he asked, smiling.

"Yes," I replied.

"Old coins, Meestair? You like? One dollar, please." I examined some of the coins, and they sure looked old to me. Now, I'm not much of a coin collector, but I know you are, Kate, so I bought a couple for you. I'll send them to you when I get back.

As he stuffed the dollar into his pocket, I pointed at the two structures I'd been studying and asked, "What are these?"

Pointing to the one on the right, he said, "Theese Zacareeah," and to the left, "theese, Avshalom."

"Zacareeah? Avshalom?" I repeated, puzzled.

"Yes, theese, tombs. Zacareeah the nabi. Avshalom, son of Dahoud." At that moment he saw a young lamb dangerously close to one of the holes in the hillside, so he threw a stone, shouted, and continued up the valley.

Zacareeah? Avshalom? Dahoud? *Who were these guys?* I wondered. (Who do *you* think they were?) It took a few moments for my mind to kick into gear. Then it hit me. Zachariah the Jewish prophet, Absalom the son of King David—these famous men were buried here! The massive structures were their monuments. I felt a sudden reverence for the history of the place. And, as I was to learn over the next few hours, reverence for history is something that overwhelms you in this city.

It's going to take me several letters to describe Israel to you. I'll take you not only through Jerusalem but to Galilee and the Red Sea as well. It should be fun!

I think it's very important for you to know that there's a big world out there. In fact, all of us need to be reminded of this from time to time. Sometimes we get so focused on our present circumstances that we forget the hugeness of the earth, the density of its population, and the depth of its history. Travel, like reading, helps put your problems in perspective.

I hope you enjoy our trip! I'll write again from Israel.

Love ya!
Uncle Bob

27 _____

Dear Jess and Kate,

Crash! It hit me last night! All the accumulated lack of sleep nearly knocked me out after I finished dinner. I collapsed on the bed without even changing into my pajamas and didn't wake up until noon. Aunt Jenny kindly let me sleep, although she couldn't resist telling me that I snored as loudly as the convoy of tanks that rumbled by last night at dinner. Now we're both out on the balcony. She's reading the *Jerusalem Post* newspaper, and I'm—guess what!—writing to my favorite niece and nephew again. Tomorrow we head for Galilee, so I want to continue the description of the long walk I took yesterday morning.

Leaving Zachariah and Absalom behind, I climbed the steep western side of the Kidron Valley, crossed the narrow road at the top, and climbed another twenty or thirty feet up to the base of the pinnacle. The first thing I did was to turn and look back at the route I'd taken.

The Kidron was so far down, and the slope so steep, that I felt like the earth was split and I might fall off. On the other side of the split was the huge hill known as the Mount of Olives. I could see the tall steeple of the Church of the Ascension at the very top. About a half-mile south of that, directly across from me, was the Intercontinental Hotel with its unique domed windows. Just a bit past the hotel, continuing south (to my right), the mountain began to slope down, and I could see just the tops of a few buildings on the edge of Bethany, a small village on the southeastern slope. In front of those buildings, at the top of the valley, was the little hotel where Aunt Jenny was still asleep.

As my eyes scanned the lower slopes of the Mount of Olives, I saw the heavily treed Garden of Gethsemane, with the walls and domes of the Church of All Nations gray in the shadow of the sunrise. Just above it and to the right was the Russian Orthodox church, with its gold-covered domes (they look like onions) glowing softly. Just a bit further to the right was the tear-shaped Dominus Flevit chapel. Then thousands of white stone graves swept down from the top of the mountain to the road winding past our hotel.

My eyes traveled north again to the next mountain, called Mount Scopus, and I saw the beautiful buildings of the Hebrew University blinking in the sunrise. To my surprise, I saw my shepherd friend and his "woolly stones" over half a mile away, climbing through the olive groves on the slope beneath the university. I waved at him; and to my utter astonishment, he waved back! Those shepherds have good eyes! (It didn't occur to me that he was probably saying to himself, "Those Americans have good eyes!")

I looked back at the pinnacle again and noticed the huge stones with which the lower part of the wall had been constructed. Some of them were six to eight feet long and two to three feet high. Obviously they had been cut out of a massive limestone cliff in a rock quarry somewhere and transported to Jerusalem by thousands of slaves. Then I saw something puzzling. The large stones went up to only about a third of the wall, and then the stones got smaller, *much* smaller. I was checking out my guidebook to see if there was an explanation for this when I heard a voice behind me say, "Do you like our city?"

I turned, somewhat surprised, and came face to face with a white-haired old gentleman whose deep blue eyes sparkled with life under bushy white eyebrows. His face was slightly red, and his bald head was glistening with perspiration. It wasn't warm enough in the early morning for these signs of physical effort, but then I saw he had a cane.

"Hello," he said in a rich British accent. "My name is Lucien Howard." He extended his hand, and I extended mine. I told him my name and that I was here on a holiday. "A beautiful morning, isn't it?" he observed. "Mind you, most mornings are like this, here in Jerusalem. But I especially love *Shabbat* mornings." He cast his eyes across the valley and said, "It's a marvelous sight. I can never get enough of it."

We walked down to the roadside. As we did so, I saw the reason for my new friend's perspiration and red face. He walked with a very pronounced limp and leaned heavily on his cane. I commented on the difficulty he must have had in climbing up to where I had been. "No. No. I do it every *Shabbat*. Love the view from that spot. That's the only vantage point where you can look north along the eastern wall, then west along the southern wall, and, in the turn of the head, see the Mount of Olives and Mount Zion. It's truly one of the finest vistas in all of the world."

I realized I was with someone who really loved Jerusalem. Yet I was thrown a bit by his accent. "Do you live here?" I asked.

"Oh, yes. Have done so since 1947. My wife and I came here as young people to help rebuild the Land." He said "Land" as if it were a living, breathing personality. His eyes gleamed with pleasure and pride as he said, "We had a bit of a battle, as you may know, but since 1948 Israel has been independent. It's a wonderful, old, so very old, yet young nation." He paused for a moment and gazed across the valley at Silwan, the Arab village growing up the hill beneath our hotel. "There's much yet to be accomplished," he said wistfully. "We still don't live in peace."

Then, changing the subject, he clapped me on the back and said, "I'm just on my way to synagogue. Care to join me?" This was an offer I couldn't refuse.

"Certainly! I'd be delighted," I answered. And we began to walk slowly along the south wall, up toward Mount Zion. As we walked, we asked and answered several questions about each other. But our conversation about ourselves was often interrupted by Lucien's descriptions of various points of interest along the way. For instance, we had barely begun when Lucien asked, "Do you see the stones in the walls, how the bottom third or so are much larger than the upper part?"

"Yes. As a matter of fact, I was just looking in my guidebook for an explanation of that very thing when we met," I said.

"King Herod laid those big ones about two thousand years ago. Then the city was razed by the Romans about seventy years later. The walls were in ruins until the Turkish emperor, Suleiman the Magnificent, rebuilt them, using those smaller stones, in the sixteenth century. Mind you," he added, "that's a very broad sketch of a very detailed history. But essentially, the present city walls are Suleiman's work."

About three hundred yards from the pinnacle, as we continued our slow walk up to Mount Zion, we stopped at a modest-looking entrance to the Old City. "That's the 'Dung Gate,' " Lucien said. "It's named that because in ancient times the garbage of the city was carried out of this gate and dumped over there." He pointed to the south, past the rooftops of houses that were almost on the same level as the road, because they were built on an unseen downward slope. "Over there, in the Hinnom Valley. You can't see it from here, but there's a very large valley just there," he pointed. "There was smoke and vile sulphur smells in the valley all the time, because of the constant burning of the refuse. In fact," he added, "you'll be interested to know that that's where the Jewish prophets got the imagery for their descriptions of hell. The valley was also called *Gehenna*—and that, of course, is one of the ancient names for hell."

"Wow! No kidding," I said, impressed.

"If you want to see the valley better, we'll get a good look at it when we're on Mount Zion. But we'd better continue on. The service will be starting soon."

We walked up the well-worn path that runs up the slope, right next to the wall. As we did so, I saw that Lucien was laboring, due to his severe limp.

"If you don't mind my asking, how did you come by that limp?" I asked. "Was it sickness or an injury?"

"An injury," he answered, puffing a bit as we came to a section of earthen stairs. "It happened during the war of 1948. I was a young soldier at Latrun, and we came under intense mortar attack. A shell landed about ten feet from me and nearly blew my leg off. I'm lucky to be alive."

"How long were you in the hospital?" I asked.

"Oh, three or four months. But it took a year before I could walk with a cane."

"How is it now? Does it hurt?"

"All the time. But I've learned something about pain. You can master it, or it can master you. It all depends on your attitude. At first I gave in to the pain and spent a lot of time feeling sorry for myself. Self-pity is a terrible thing, you know." He stopped to wipe his face with a bandanna. "It exaggerates everything negative. You envy others. You put them down. You put yourself down. And the pain has a heyday with your body. It runs rampant, instead of staying in its own neighborhood."

"What do you mean," I asked, fascinated, "by 'neighborhood'?"

"I mean this: have you ever sat out on a peaceful summer evening, and some little bug flies past your peripheral field of vision? You don't focus on it, but your brain tells you that you saw it. Now, you hate mosquitoes, right?"

"Sure do. So does everyone."

"So true. Well, something in your brain tells you the bug was a mosquito. Suddenly you find yourself scratching here, slapping there. Within minutes you feel like you've been bitten twenty times. When, in fact, there are no mosquitoes at all."

"So?"

"So, that's what I mean. For a long time I let the pain in my leg run to all parts of my body. My brain said, 'You're injured,' so my whole body started aching here, throbbing there, until I realized what was going on. Then I put my pain in its place. Since then, my leg hurts, but the rest of me is one hundred percent."

"That's why you walk all this way every Sabbath?" I ventured.

"Exactly. Every step hurts my leg. But the rest of me is inspired! And it does my leg good anyway, in spite of its complaints," he chuckled. "Oh, look! Here's the Zion Gate."

Together we looked at the beautiful structure. It was quite narrow—maybe twelve feet wide—and quite high; I'd guess twenty feet. It was artistically outlined in carved stone and had a weathered, regal presence. But there was something strange about it too. The entire gate was covered with hundreds of indentations that made it look like it was suffering from a stone version of terminal acne! I turned to Lucien; but before I could ask, he answered, "Bullet holes, they're from the War of Independence. It was a vicious, deadly battle for the Old City. Most of the battle was waged right here, where we're standing. Believe it or not, most of those bullets were fired by Israelis."

"How come?" I asked.

"Because the Old City was held by the Jordanians. They fought with great dedication from within the walls. We had to break through. In fact," and he started to walk a few steps past the gate, "look at this." He pointed at a fairly small indentation in the wall just above ground level. "That's where we tried to break the wall with a large explosive device." He laughed. "Didn't do much damage, did it?"

Then, looking at his watch, he said, "Uh-oh. We're a bit late. Mind you, being on time is a relative term in this country."

With that we walked through the Zion Gate and into the Jewish Quarter of Jerusalem. In the next letter I'll tell you about the synagogue service and my visit to the famous "Wailing Wall" down near the Dung Gate.

Much love to you both,
Uncle Bob

28   ✍

Dear Jess and Kate,

It's early morning again. In a few hours Aunt Jenny and I will be checking out of the hotel and driving to the Sea of Galilee. She's still asleep—same old story! So I'm out here on the balcony, where I want to finish describing my walk through Jerusalem. *Through* is not exactly the right word. *Over* is more like it. You'll see why after I tell you about the synagogue service.

The Zion Gate forces you to turn east when you enter, because the inside passage is a very short and abrupt right angle leading to the right. You come out of the gate (which is much like a mini-tunnel) facing east along the inside of the southern wall. On your left is a row of shops; on the right is the wall; and straight ahead, over a long cobblestone road and the southern end of a parking lot, you can see all the way to the Mount of Olives on the horizon. Lucien and I walked down the cobblestone road to the edge of the full parking lot. As we were walking around it, Lucien said, "There won't be too much action here today. Most of us don't drive on *Shabbat*."

"Why not?" I asked.

"Because there's a law in the Bible about not starting fires on *Shabbat*. A car engine operates on internal combustion, right? Combustion is fire. So the rabbis determined way back when the car was invented that *Shabbat* was a day to park, not to drive. I rather like it. So does Jerusalem, I think," he said, looking to the sky. "It clears the air."

We turned down a narrow street and left the openness of the parking area behind. It was like plunging into a lake and swimming beneath the surface. The Old City is another world, as different from the outside world as underwater is from above water. The narrowness of the streets, the offshooting alleyways, the little shops, the unending closeness of home to home, the texture of the stone, the earthy smell of dust, the buildings rising row on row above, shutting out the sky—all these things instantly immerse you in an atmosphere that balances the richest history of any city on earth with the raw political and sensitive religious realities that only Jerusalem can call out of the heart of mankind. We walked silently, as reverently as if we were entering a holy sanctuary. The only sound in the still morning was the tapping of Lucien's cane.

One street to the right, another to the left, straight ahead for a hundred feet or so, then left again. Suddenly we were at the top of an old stone stairway that led down to a low building with small windows on either side of the door. When I use the word *building*, I may be misleading you—I know how active your imaginations are, and I'm sure you're drawing pictures in your minds as you read my descriptions. The synagogue was not so much a building as it was a part of a building. And that "building" is the entire Old City. Apart from a few very old churches and a mosque or synagogue or two, there are very few free-standing buildings. They all blend into one another and share common walls and roofs. In fact, the flat roof of this synagogue was at street level, and there were tables set on it outside a small cafe. There were no customers, however. Not only was it the Sabbath (there was a CLOSED sign in the window), but it was just seven o'clock in the morning.

As we walked down the stairs, a boy suddenly bounded out of the synagogue doorway. "*Sabba*," he cried, and threw his arms around Lucien's middle.

"Avi! How are you? So great to see you! *Shabbat Shalom*," Lucien said.

"*Shabbat Shalom* to you too, Grandpa. Are you coming in now? You're the last man for the *minyan*."

"Yep. Right away. But first meet my new friend from America." He introduced us and told me that *Sabba* meant "Grandpa" and that Avi had English-speaking parents, who, of course, also spoke Hebrew.

"Avi is twelve," Lucien said.

"Twelve and a half," Avi corrected him.

"Oh, yes," Lucien laughed, "twelve and a half, and almost a man! In six months he will be bar mitzvahed, and he will be able to join the prayers. But for the time being, he just watches the service. Say! Why don't you sit with him during the service, and he'll give you a play-by-play description? What do you say, Avi?"

"Sure, Sabba, that'd be great!" Looking me straight in the eye, he said, "C'mon in. You sit with me. Grandpa's got to join the *minyan*."

"What's a *minyan*?" I asked, feeling ignorant.

"Oh. That's a group of ten men. You can't start a service without a *minyan*. Grandpa's number ten this morning. They're anxious to start. Let's go!"

I must say I was a bit shocked when I went inside. I was expecting something ornate and churchlike. Instead, it was just a small, plain room with a few backless benches and a piece of furniture that looked like a cupboard with a faded red curtain on its front. The small windows provided most of the light, although some did come from the open door. There was also one bare light bulb hanging by a thin wire from the plastered ceiling, but it wasn't working. The air was stale, and the stone floor was cool. The walls, which felt a bit damp, had no pictures. It was a dull room. But it was full of color.

The men were the colorful ones. Each of them, including Lucien, was wearing a plain but beautiful white prayer shawl with fringes at the ends. Most of the shawls had blue or black stripes running parallel to the edges, and they were draped over the men's heads and shoulders, hanging right down to their waists. Avi told me that a man's head had to be covered before he could worship in a synagogue. That's why he had a small black skullcap on his head. Even I had on a brown construction-paper cap, which someone had given me as I entered.

"But where are the women?" I asked.

"Women don't worship with us. If they happen to attend, which is seldom, they sit behind that screen over there." He pointed at a folding screen leaning against the wall in the back corner. "In some of the other synagogues they let the women join them. But not ours."

I was just about to ask, "Why not?" when the service began. The men began to sing, and someone parted the curtains on the cupboard, revealing a large scroll. He took it out and each man kissed it. A few took a corner of their shawls, kissed the shawl, and then touched the scroll with it. As they did that, I noticed that they had black strips of leather wrapped around their arms and small black boxes attached to their foreheads.

"What's that?" (meaning the scroll), I whispered. "And what are those?" (meaning the strips and boxes).

"That's the Torah—the Law of Moses—and those strips of leather have some of the Law written on them."

"And the boxes?"

"They have some of the Law in them too."

"How come?"

"The Bible says we're to attach the law to our forearms and our foreheads."

"Why are they kissing the scroll?"

"Respect."

For the next hour or so, the men took turns reading the scroll in a kind of singsong. I couldn't understand a word, because the words were all in Hebrew, but the service was a joy to watch. There was tremendous love and respect in their movements as they prayed, their voices as they read, and their hands as they handled the Word of God. I was greatly moved.

As the service was about to end, I asked Avi a question that had been bothering me for the past hour. "Where's the rabbi?"

"They're all rabbis."

"Even your grandfather?"

"Uh-huh."

"So who's in charge?"

"All of them."

In those three words I gained a real insight into Israeli life. Israel may have a prime minister, political parties (over thirty of them!), and a huge bureaucracy. But in the final analysis, no one in Israel sees himself as a follower. In Israel everyone is a leader. It all starts with a *minyan*.

After the service, Lucien and Avi walked outside with me. "So what's happening now?" Lucien asked.

"Well, I thought I'd like to see a bit more of the city," I answered.

"Say! I have an idea," Lucien said. "Avi, why don't you take Bob for a tour? You know the city very well."

"Sure," Avi answered with excitement. "I'd *love* to do that!" And, after I promised Lucien that Aunt Jenny and I would come to his house for tea when we returned to Jerusalem from Eilat, Avi and I were off. What happened next will always be one of my most treasured memories.

Within moments we were in a maze of narrow streets and alleyways. Suddenly Avi darted into a passage so narrow that both my shoulders scraped the walls as I followed him. At the end of the passage there was a steep stone staircase.

"Follow me!" Avi whispered, almost in a conspiratorial tone.

"Where are we going?" I asked.

"Up on the roof," he answered. "We're gonna take the roofs."

"Why are we whispering?" I grunted, as we climbed the stairs.

"Because the woman who lives in this house hangs her laundry on the roof, and if she's up there, she'll shout and scream and try to kick us off."

"Well, maybe we shouldn't—"

"Nah! No problem. We'll get by her. And once we do, it's clear sailing from here on."

To my relief, she wasn't there. I was feeling like a thief already. But my guilt feelings quickly vanished—in fact, my breath was taken away—as we came out on the roof.

The Old City swept down from our vantage point like a bedspread on a rumpled mattress. It had hills and valleys, and an attractive disorder made it look like a patchwork quilt of flat, rounded, black, white, tiled, gray, steepled, domed, harsh, soft, pointed, old, new, organized confusion. The jumble was bordered by Suleiman's wall. On the horizon was the entire Mount of Olives and Mount Scopus skyline, in all its sun-risen splendor.

For the next two hours we climbed down, climbed up, jumped, crawled, and scrambled all over the top of Jerusalem. We saw shopkeepers opening their shops in the Christian and Arab quarters, women sweeping their doorsteps, children playing football in the streets, and orthodox Jewish men walking to and from their synagogues. We saw the three main religious sites for the three great world religions: the Christian Church of the Holy Sepulcher, the Moslem Dome of the Rock, and the Jewish Western (or Wailing) Wall. It was quite a sight looking down on hundreds of black-coated men bobbing as they prayed at the wall. And we could plainly hear their prayers, some of which could definitely be described as *wailing*.

In the course of our adventure, we saw the seven gates of Jerusalem: Zion, Jaffa, New, Damascus, Herod's, Lion's, and Dung. My favorite was the Damascus Gate. It was ornately decorated with beautiful black and white rock that gave it an almost castlelike look. We even hopped from some roofs onto the wall from time to time and were able to look out at the morning traffic beginning to flow in, out, and around the city.

One of the highlights was a talk we had with an Israeli soldier who was stationed on the wall above the Western Wall. It was fascinating to talk with someone who had been a tank commander in the Six-Day War.

Needless to say, I didn't want this experience to end. But at around 9:30 A.M. Avi told me he had to go. He took me to a staircase built into the wall near the Lion's gate. After promising each other that we'd meet again at Grandpa Lucien's house in a few days, we parted. I bought a bagel and a soft drink from a vendor at the gate, glowing in the joy I had just experienced. A few minutes later, I walked the road that skirts the Garden of Gethsemane, returning to the hotel just as Aunt Jenny was wiping the sleep from her eyes.

It's time for Aunt Jenny and me to go. I'll write from Tiberias.

Lots of love,
Uncle Bob

29

Dear Jess and Kate,

Hi! How are you doing? Want to know what I'm doing? You guessed it. I'm on another balcony, this time at a hotel in Tiberias, on the shore of the Sea of Galilee. When we arrived here this afternoon, Aunt Jenny and I were very surprised to see that this "sea" is really nothing more than a small freshwater lake. It's only about twelve miles long and six miles wide, small by our North American standards, right? But its history is anything but small. In fact, compared to America's two centuries, its history is absolutely huge! More armies, emperors, kings, and generals have camped on its shores than on any other lake in recorded time. It has seen the rise and fall of empires and has witnessed the writing of the gigantic Jewish Talmud and the earth-shaking ministry of Jesus of Nazareth. While armies have clashed on its surrounding hills and prophets have preached on its stony beaches, the fishermen have faithfully put out their nets, and *Kinneret* (as Israelis call it) has gone on, feeding its dependent families and shimmering in the sunlight.

Even though it has this sense of history and holiness about it, the Sea of Galilee is certainly in tune with the times. Aunt Jenny and I drove all around it today and saw three very modern water-slide parks, gorgeous resort hotels, thriving campsites, and people sailing, Windsurfing, and water-skiing on its deep blue waters.

At the south end of the lake, not far from one of the water parks, is the beginning of the Jordan River. Like Galilee, the Jordan has a rich history. Nevertheless, it meets very modern needs as it wanders down to the Dead Sea, providing vital water for the irrigation of fields in the Jordan Valley. Those fields, by the way, are owned by Jordanian farmers on the east side of the river, and Israelis on the west. Both countries, as you may know, have a dim view of each other. But on either side of the Jordan, the farmers share the water and the sun and live in peace.

As I sit here on this balcony, the Sea of Galilee is asleep, and the sky is black. Everything is so dark, in fact, that the lights of the *kibbutzim,* across the lake on the Golan Heights, look like they're floating in the sky. It's quite a sight. To the east and the north, it looks like there are hundreds of planes in the sky, with their landing lights on. The only difference is that the lights are stationary. It almost seems that I'm at the bottom of a massive dark basin with bright stars on the rim. As you might expect, it's totally silent right now. All I can hear is the gentle lapping of the water on the shore.

While driving down from Jerusalem through the Judean desert this morning, Aunt Jenny and I were listening to the BBC on the car radio. One of the news items was about a prominent British rock star who had just committed suicide. "His suicide followed several months of depression," the report said. This news made me think of Howard Hummer, who, after losing his family in that wreck, came close to doing the same.

As you might expect, with the loss of his family, everything changed for Howard. For one thing, he couldn't go back to the farm, which meant living in someone else's home and eating someone else's food. For another, his entire daily routine was upset. Previously, he had awakened every morning at 5:00 A.M.; gone out to the barn to help his dad with the chores; had a full, hot breakfast, lovingly prepared by his mom; and saddled old Nellie, riding to school by 8:30. Before the accident, he attended a wonderful little country school with a group of other farm kids as schoolmates. Now he was right across the street from the school in town. In fact, living in the Shultzes' home meant he was close to everything—neighbors, school, stores, and people. He was used to the isolation of a farm. In town he felt closed in, trapped, and suffocated, almost as if he'd moved to another world. He felt foreign and out of step. Nothing was the same.

Howard's only comfort in this black new world was a scruffy, stray Labrador dog named Napoleon. Nobody in town knew where he'd come from. He just appeared one day and stayed.

Napoleon lived on the outer fringes of town life. He was always there, mind you, at all town events—weddings, funerals, Sunday school picnics, baseball games, and whatever else attracted a crowd. The townspeople came to expect to see him at all public gatherings. If for some reason he was late or didn't show up, someone would say, "I wonder where Napoleon is?"

When Napoleon did show up, his arrival was always undoglike and dignified. He didn't do the sniff-everything-and-everyone stuff; nor did he head straight for the food, if it was an outdoor picnic or barbecue. Rather, he would quietly sit on his haunches on the edge of the crowd and watch everything with intelligent, dark brown eyes. He was kind to children and would tolerate their petting and tackling with an unruffled stateliness. He never wagged his tail or growled at anyone. Whenever someone brought or left food for him to eat, he would wait until everyone was gone before dining. He preferred to eat alone.

He also preferred to live alone. His home was a ditch or a culvert. In the summer he slept in a ditch—in the winter, a culvert. Often in winter the townspeople would see him stiffly emerging from his culvert, so frost-covered that he looked like "the ghost of Christmas past." His first morning ritual was an elaborate and painful-looking stretching routine. Then, after loosening up, he would give himself a thorough shaking and proceed to his regular patrol of events. If there wasn't much happening, he tended to spend his time at Bulman's blacksmith shop, where he could add his silent presence to the daily conversations.

There was one thing, however, that unraveled Napoleon's dignity every time. He could not resist a fast-moving car. He snubbed slow cars. But speeding cars? When one went past, he would take after it like a rocket. He wouldn't bark or snap at the tires like dogs of lesser mettle. He'd simply race it, with a look of intense concentration and commitment, as though he were testing himself. If a few days went by without a worthy opponent, he was often seen outside of town at the railroad tracks, waiting to chase the train. When the race was done, he would walk away with a smile on his face. That smile was the only show of emotion he allowed himself. But it was enough. He was a dog with a passion for life.

Perhaps this was why Napoleon immediately took an interest in Howard. From his doggy point of view, Howard was a stray too—a sudden stranger without any sense of roots. What's more, as the Shultzes and the schoolteacher soon began to realize, Howard was losing his will to live. Napoleon somehow must have sensed this. He and Howard soon became fast friends. In fact, Howard's only friend in the whole town was this silent, wise, passionate dog. They were seen everywhere together. Howard and Napoleon seemed to have an understanding.

It was Mrs. Shultz who first noticed that Howard was losing his appetite and growing thinner every day. She tried to press food on the boy, but Howard would push it away, saying, "I'm not hungry." The teacher saw his marks slipping as his ability to concentrate eroded. He spent a lot of time in class either daydreaming or dozing. She suspected that he wasn't getting enough sleep. And she was right. Howard was finding it more and more difficult to fall asleep. And when he did, it was a fitful, light sleep that brought no rest. His emotions were on edge as well. He was easily angered and easily discouraged. He would weep at the slightest upset and lash out at the slightest provocation. Howard didn't know it, but he was in a depression. His sense of detachment from life and his eroding will to live were dangerous signals that his depression had reached a serious stage. Unless he got help, he would soon become suicidal.

Over time, that's exactly what happened. Winter had given way to a glorious spring. Everyone was remarking on how wonderful the weather was. Everyone was happy and full of life. Everyone, that is, except Howard. He couldn't understand how the others could be so happy. He couldn't understand how anybody could laugh or have a good time. His earlier sense of suffocation gave way to a different, dangerous form of isolation. For him, there was no sun in the sky, no joy—just blackness and meaningless-ness. He was beyond bitterness, anger, or sorrow. He was empty and had no reason to live. One especially black Saturday night he decided to end it all. Tomorrow would be his thirteenth birthday, and it would be his last day on earth.

Strangely, this decision gave him a sense of purpose, and he slept well that night. Early the next morning, before the Shultzes got up, he left the house and walked over a mile to the railway crossing. He had decided to throw himself in front of the train at the very spot where his family had died.

When he got there, he saw the smoke puffing from the steam engine about a half-mile away. He had just a few minutes to live. He felt no fear. He felt no excitement. He'd left no note. This was not a cry for help or some grandstand attempt for attention. He was deadly serious. The train was now about a quarter-mile away, moving at about twenty-five miles an hour. "Should be enough," Howard said to himself coldly. Now it was two hundred yards, now one hundred, now fifty, now . . .

Suddenly, as Howard jumped onto the tracks, there was a black blur in the ditch beside the train. It was Napoleon, chasing the steam engine, a look of grim determination and wild abandon in his eyes. In a matter of milliseconds, the wise old stray assessed the situation. Without hesitation he sped past the puffing locomotive, leaped, and hit Howard full force, square in the chest, knocking the boy off the tracks. There was a faint thud and yelp of pain as the train rumbled past. Howard was alive. Napoleon was dead.

The train was gone as quickly as it had come. Howard sat up beside the tracks. On the other side, he saw Napoleon lying lifeless in the grass. With his heart aching and his eyes stinging, Howard dug a shallow grave for Napoleon with his hands. As he gently smoothed the last of the sand over Napoleon's body, he lifted his head to the sky and released a heart-rending cry of sorrow. Then he stood and walked back to town. He didn't look back. Napoleon had given him a new life. From that day until today, seventy-seven years later, Howard Hummer is still going straight ahead. Since Napoleon's heroic self-sacrifice, and in spite of many ups and downs, Howard has never lacked inspiration or purpose. He's a man with a passion for life.

Jess and Kate, you need to know that everybody experiences depression, to a greater or lesser degree. If that depression is deep enough, some of us have thoughts of suicide. Occasional meaninglessness and emptiness seem to be part of the ingredients of life's recipe. You'll probably face it sooner or later. When you do, remember Napoleon.

Love ya,
Uncle Bob

30

Dear Jess and Kate,

I'm sitting beside the pool at our hotel in Eilat, feeling lucky to be alive. My hands are still shaking. Do I have a story to tell you today! It all started three days ago when Aunt Jenny and I decided to spend a day in Egypt.

I was going to tell you about our tour of the Galilee area and our visit to Nazareth, Capernaum, Metulla, and Mount Hermon. But in light of what happened yesterday, I think I'll save the tour description for a later time when we can visit and show you our videos.

When we arrived in Eilat, we checked in at the same time as a busload of Israelis. They were a group of expatriates who all spoke English. In fact, when I heard them talking and visiting in the hotel lobby, I thought they were a group of Americans. But then I saw them presenting Israeli passports to the registrar. They were on their way to Egypt the next day.

That night Aunt Jenny and I were a few minutes late for dinner in the hotel dining room. (She needed extra time to put makeup over her sunburn!) When we got there all the tables were filled, most of them with people from the Israeli tour group. The headwaiter was about to put out an extra table when one of the Israelis, who was sitting at a table for four, got up, came over to us, smiled, and said, "Why don't you join us? There's just my wife and I at our table." We accepted his invitation a bit shyly, but gladly. I was famished!

Our new friends introduced themselves. His name was Gilad Even-Ari, an Israeli of German descent, whose family had lived in Jerusalem for four generations. He was a lawyer who specialized in international law and had several multinational corporations as clients. His wife, Mandy, was from Canada. She had come to Israel for two weeks, twenty years ago, just to please her rabbi father. She'd fallen in love with the country, then with Gilad, and had never left. Within a half-hour or so, we felt like we'd known them for years.

Gilad told us that the tour group was leaving the next day for Saint Catherine's in the Sinai peninsula. "We'll cross the border at Taba; an Egyptian tour bus will meet us; and three hours later we'll be there," he said.

"Why do you have to change buses?" I asked.

"That's the way it is in this part of the world," Mandy answered. "It cuts down on terrorism."

"Terrorism? On buses?" I asked, amazed.

"Sure. Unfortunately, it's happened quite a few times. Tour buses with Israelis on them are quite a target for any small terrorist group trying to make a name for itself. But, hey! It's not going to happen. And, if it did, the terrorists would have a handful with this group," Gilad said.

Mandy laughed. "Believe it. This whole group is made up of British, Canadian, and American Israelis who have served with the Golani Brigade. These guys are animals!"

"The Golani Brigade?" Aunt Jenny asked.

"Yeah. They're the Israeli equivalent of the American Navy Seals. These guys were part of one of the greatest SWAT teams in the world. Now they're retired, but they still do forty days of reserve duty every year. You wouldn't want to mess with them!" said Mandy.

"Or with their wives," added Gilad. "Many of them were in the army as young women and know how to handle everything from guns to grenades. Yes, sir! This is quite the group!"

At this point our dinner arrived. We ate and talked for the next twenty minutes. Then, as we had cake and coffee, I asked, "Why are you going to the Sinai desert?"

"Well, first of all, we love it. It's absolutely gorgeous. Have you been there?" Gilad asked.

"No. But we'd like to see it. Maybe next time."

"Why not this time?" Gilad asked.

"Well, uh, we didn't plan to. And, well, I'm not sure we could arrange it in the few days we have till our return to the States," I answered.

"So what's to arrange?" Gilad asked with a shrug of his shoulders. "You'll come with us. We've had one couple cancel, so we've got room, both on the bus and in the hotel at Saint Catherine's. We leave tomorrow at 10 A.M. What do you think?"

Aunt Jenny and I looked at each other, and I could see the "Why not?" in her eyes. "Why not?" I said with a grin. "We'd love to."

"Fantastic! You're gonna enjoy the trip and the climb."

"The climb?"

"Oh, didn't I tell you? We're climbing Mount Sinai the day after tomorrow at two in the morning. We're going to see a sunrise to end all sunrises! Man, are you in for a treat!"

As we went to bed that night, Aunt Jenny and I wondered what we'd gotten ourselves into. But we were excited and didn't sleep too well. Tomorrow we'd be off on an unexpected adventure, as guests of the Golani Brigade. Who ever would have thought it?

Eilat is Israel's southernmost city, famous for its resort atmosphere and outstanding coral reefs. It feels more like a European Riviera town than a Middle Eastern city, and it attracts sun seekers and scuba divers from all over the world. Just about four miles south of the main street is the border crossing into Egypt. The only thing on the other side of the border is a luxury hotel and some low, run-down customs buildings. This is Taba.

We stopped at the Taba crossing about fifteen minutes after 10:00 the next morning. An hour later, the endless paperwork all done, we crossed into Egypt and transferred to the Egyptian bus. The narrow road followed the coast for the first half of the trip. On the left we could see the deep blue of the Red Sea, on the right the wildly textured colors of desert mountains and plains. About two hours from Taba we turned inland and began traveling southwest, into the mountains.

After one very tough fifteen-minute climb in first gear, the bus stopped at the top, and we all piled out to take a look at the view. As we looked out over the tops of mountains and through the canyons below us, with the Red Sea on the horizon, a couple of the men went over behind a juniper bush for a minor watering ritual. They were well within sight, although veiled somewhat by the bush, but no one seemed to notice. Aunt Jenny and I have been amazed time and again at how casual Middle Easterners are about these delicate matters. Why, one day we saw a mother assisting her son as he watered a tree on Ben Yehuda street in Jerusalem, using his own self-made supply!

Just beyond the bush was a Bedouin tent. The Bedouins, as you may know, are desert dwellers. They live in sprawling tents made of black goat hair and usually have herds of goats. (Wealthy Bedouins have herds of camels.) This family had goats. Even as two young Bedouins came toward us to sell some trinkets, one of the goats ran past them, right at the two men watering the bush. He was a big, mean-looking, oily-haired ram, with fire in his eyes.

He took aim at one of the men and butted him in the backside with an angry bellow, using such force that he sent the man sprawling. One of the Bedouins ran over, issuing loud commands, and subdued the ram before he was able to flatten the other guy. In Hebrew the other Bedouin apologized and said they usually had the ram tied up because he would attack anybody, including them, if they happened to stray near that bush. Seems he was protecting his turf. Gilad told me later that the Bedouin called the goat "Faisal." He laughed, "It's unusual to give a goat a name, but I guess that one's such a character, he's taken on his own personality."

Ha! Faisal the goat! Can you believe it! Ha, ha, ha! We all had a good laugh as the bus drove on, with one exception. He was sitting crookedly on his seat, staring out the window.

We had gone about ten miles when it happened. The bus had just climbed a short, steep hill when it came to a sudden, tire-screeching halt. We were nearly thrown from our seats. We looked out and saw the reason for our sudden stop. There were three Bedouins standing across the road. They were wearing flowing black robes and had their faces covered with bright, checkered *kaffiyas*. All three were pointing machine guns at the driver. They motioned for him to open the door and come out. Sweating profusely, he did so, his hands high above his head. After a couple of minutes of loud commands and threatening gestures, they ordered him back on the bus. The poor man stumbled up the stairs and told us they wanted to talk to someone in Arabic. Gilad volunteered immediately, and the two of them went out to hear the terrorists' demands.

While Gilad was negotiating, the Golanis in the bus were totally silent, watching the proceedings with intense concentration. They showed no fear. Rather, they showed focus—cold, calculating focus. As the minutes raced on, I finally couldn't take it anymore and blurted out, "What are you guys gonna do? You're Golanis, right? You should be able to handle those three."

"In most cases, yes," the one across the aisle from us said. "But in this case it's complicated."

"How come?"

"Look at the smallest one, the guy on the right. He's got explosives tied around his waist. See the bulge under his robes? Suicide bombers are impossible to control. He's just a kid. Looks nervous as heck."

I looked. Sure enough, he did have a bulge, and he did look nervous. He kept looking around, fingering the trigger of his gun.

Finally Gilad and the driver came back onto the bus, all three terrorists behind them. They stood at the front, their guns pointing at us, while Gilad spoke. "They want us to turn around and drive back to Taba. They plan to ram the gate at the border. When we cross into Israel they intend to blow us all up—including themselves. If anybody tries to interfere between here and there they'll blow us up on the spot. There's to be no talk and no heroes."

The driver turned the bus around, and we headed back toward Taba. Everything was deadly calm. The only noise was the considerable sound of the bus engine and the wind blowing in the open windows. There was very little if any emotion on the faces of the hostages. The only one on the bus who betrayed any lack of composure was the boy with the explosives. Several times over the next few miles he would speak to the leader, and the leader would angrily deny him whatever he was asking for. But as the minutes passed he kept at it, till there was a great deal of urgency to his request. The Golani across the aisle caught my eye and silently mouthed the words, "The kid has a digestive problem," giving me a slight smile and a wink. I couldn't believe he saw this as funny!

Personally, I felt like I had a digestive problem. My insides were churning with anxiety. Aunt Jenny, however, seemed as calm as the Israelis. "Are that kid and I the only cowards on this bus?" I asked myself. The whole event was becoming nightmarish.

Eventually the boy won. The leader spoke harshly to the driver, and the bus pulled over to the side of the road. I looked out, and we'd stopped exactly where we'd been an hour ago. There was the Bedouin tent—and there was Faisal's juniper bush!

The boy rushed off the bus, gathering his robes up to his waist, even as he ran. In his urgency he made a critical mistake. He ran behind the juniper.

He had just squatted, his robes thrown up over his head, when Faisal appeared. The boy was facing us as he performed his urgent task, so he didn't see the ram pawing the ground, plotting his trajectory. Even as the boy dealt with a trajectory of a different sort, Faisal reared up on his hind legs like a sprinter and took off, the young terrorist in his fiery sights. He hit him with such force that we could hear the splat on the bus. The boy cartwheeled into the bush and dangled there in a most indecorous manner. The other two terrorists, distracted momentarily by this unexpected spectacle, suddenly found themselves overpowered by quick-thinking Golanis. In a matter of moments all three were facedown on the ground, their eyes wide with terror. A bus load of anti-terrorists had just been saved by a goat.

The real ordeal was what happened next. You wouldn't believe what we had to go through over the next ten hours! Three hours of waiting, questioning, and shouting and screaming among the officials followed. The border crossing was much more of a nightmare than the hostage-taking had been. Frankly, even though we didn't see Mount Sinai, I don't think I'll ever want to go to Egypt again. The bureaucracy there is almost its own form of terrorism!

But, then again, if we hadn't gone we never would have met Faisal. I'll never forget his look of regal triumph as he sauntered away from his victory. I wonder if he'll ever know that he's a hero?

You know what? That's the way it usually turns out. The one who has been prepared for heroic acts rarely becomes a hero. It's the guy, or goat, who just does what comes naturally in a very unnatural situation who proves to be the hero. As is usually the case with true heroes, they seem to be the only ones who don't appear to be too impressed with the importance of what they've accomplished. They just saunter away.

Fun story huh? We're flying back to the United States tomorrow. It will be good to be home again!

Love,
Uncle Bob

31

Dear Jess and Kate,

Your mom called last night and told us about that terrible fight at your neighbor's house on the weekend. She said you were both very upset by the violence and that you have been sleeping in her room ever since. I don't blame you. I'm upset too, just hearing about it. I think it was you, Kate, who asked why some fathers, "when they leave their wives and children, keep coming back to yell at and beat up their families and make everyone cry. Why don't they just stay away?" you wanted to know. Your mom said she didn't think she had given you a very good answer. So she asked me to give it some thought and put it in this letter. Well, I *have* given it some thought, and here's how I see it.

First of all, I think this incident has given you a very powerful message. Even though your dad has left, he has not harassed or haunted you by showing up unannounced with threats and violence. He has treated you and your mom with respect and kept his distance. You're very fortunate; a lot of kids whose parents divorce never know any peace. Their dads become enemies.

But getting back to your question, Kate, why do fathers who leave sometimes come back to threaten and hurt their former wives and children? I think the answer lies in one word: *control.* Let me explain what I mean.

Most abusers grew up abused themselves. They not only saw their fathers abusing their mothers and brothers and sisters, but they themselves were victims. Their young bodies and minds were imprinted with an overwhelming image: fathers are people who yell, curse, rage, and lash out at those smaller and weaker than themselves. As victims they absorbed the punishment, often with tears of confusion. As growing boys they began to look to the day when they could finally release their rage—when they would become abusers themselves. As often as they could while growing up, they would abuse anything weaker or smaller, like their pet dog, the girls at school, or the skinny little boys in the neighborhood. They became bullies.

Their bullying was more than a reaction to the pain at home or a reflection of their family model. It was their way of feeling secure. You see, when you're little and there's a raging adult male looking to punch and kick you, you run and hide. Most abused kids spend a lot of time under beds, in closets, or out late at night, just to avoid the beatings. In their fear they are painfully aware that they have absolutely no control over their lives. The abusive father completely controls them by his strength and his rage.

But when they're at school or on the playground, and there are smaller and weaker kids around, they can turn the tables and use their strength and size to terrorize these little ones. For a moment or two they feel the security of being in control. (They feel strong and tough just like their fathers.) Mind you, if they have any decency at all, they also feel the regret and scuzziness of knowing that they have done a hateful thing. But that sense of control is like a drug. It gives a much-needed sense of security. It's a false security; but someone who grows up without any at all will settle for almost any counterfeit.

So these bullies grow up, marry, and have kids; and the cycle of violence continues. Aunt Jenny and I were discussing this a few hours ago, and she said, "I wonder why women marry guys like that? Surely they know what they're getting into?" Yes, I suppose they do—and that's what makes it so sad. Too often these women were abused as children, and their view of marriage and home includes rage and violence from a dominant male. They say that boys tend to marry someone like their mothers and that girls tend to marry someone like their fathers. Sadly, this seems to be true with many kids who grow up in an abusive home. Strangely, the violence that makes the husband secure as an abuser makes the wife secure as the abused. It's a tragic and sick reality.

Something happens, however, when that abused woman becomes a mother. It was one thing to be hit by a husband; it's another thing to see him hit your baby. Suddenly she becomes protective and fights back. This makes the violence even worse, and the marriage tends to break up. Then the husband leaves.

Generally he leaves only for a while. He comes back, promising he'll never do it again. When she takes him back, in no time he's beating her and the kids again. She throws him out. He comes back. He becomes violent. And he's gone again. It's a vicious cycle.

While these men are away, they often do a strange thing. They *stalk* their wives and kids. This means that they sneak around following their family. They're almost like wild animals looking for prey. Your mom tells me that's what was happening at your neighbor's. Apparently he had begun parking his car out on the street and peering through the windows of the house. The woman confronted him on the weekend and called the police; and the fight began.

Why do these men stalk? They do it because they want to control their families. If they can't control from within the house, they'll control at a distance. And they do it because it's the only thing that makes them feel secure. It's sad, it's sick, and it's what a lot of kids from separated and divorced families have to live with every day of their lives.

Again, I want to say how fortunate you are that your father is not an abuser and a stalker. It hurts you, your mom, and us to know that he wants to live on his own. But thank God every day that he loves you, even though he chooses not to live with you. It could be worse. Much worse.

Well, this has been a rather serious letter. I wish I were closer to you so that I could come over and just hug you.

I think I'll sign off for now. But I'll be hugging you in my dreams.

Uncle Bob

32   ✍

Dear Jess and Kate,

For some time I've been wanting to tell you about one of my most special memories from that summer at Manitoulin Island when I nearly died in the fire. It's a memory that I truly treasure. It all started the day David Hummer brought his dad, Howard, to meet me.

When they arrived at Rainbow Village I was just getting ready to take my little dinghy out for some fishing. I had my fishing pole, worms, tackle box, and stringer already in the boat. I had just gone to get my fishing hat from our cottage when I heard David's pick-up truck roll onto the grounds. He honked the horn, stuck his head out the window, waved, and shouted, "Hi, Bobby! Come and meet my dad!" I ran over just as this grizzled bear of a man emerged from the passenger door. His deep blue eyes twinkled kindly as he extended his hand and said, "How are you doing, son?" I was astonished at the strength of his grip.

I looked up at him with keen interest, trying to see the twelve-year-old orphan in this hulking figure of a man. But there was nothing boyish, weak, or vulnerable about him. He was about six and a half feet tall and had the most massive chest and shoulders I'd ever seen. (David told me later that if you put a tape measure around Howard's chest, back, and shoulders, the measurement was sixty-six inches. That's *five and a half feet!*) He had no visible waist; rather, he was what Uncle Bill called *barrel-chested.* His upper body, from hips to shoulders, was shaped like a huge oak barrel, with heavy arms and legs sticking out in the appropriate places. He had no neck to speak of. His shoulders seemed to slope up to his ears. And the best way to describe his head was *beautiful* and *lion-like.* He had chiseled features like a sculpture, with flowing hair and a curly beard, sprinkled liberally with gray. He reminded me of a picture I had once seen of a powerful old lion roaring loudly at the setting sun on the plains of Africa. Howard Hummer was awesome.

David saw me admiring his dad and said, "Dad's come up to the island for a few weeks. He just arrived yesterday—wants to go fishin'."

"He does?" I said to David. Then, turning immediately to Howard, I said, "You do?"

"Yep. Sure do. My gear's in the back of the truck," he said.

"So why don't you come with me?" I asked enthusiastically. "I'm goin' out right now!"

"Perfect," David exclaimed. "I've got to go to Gore Bay for a few hours. Why don't you go with Bobby, and I'll pick you up on the way back?"

"Great!" said Howard, as he went out to the back of the truck to get his stuff. "Let's go, Bobby! Have you got any worms? I've got lots."

It took only a moment to realize that we'd never be able to go out in my little dinghy. Howard was just too big. So we shifted our gear to a bigger rowboat that Uncle Bill and I often used for fishing, and we were on our way. Well, almost. Howard, who was to do the rowing, gave such a mighty pull with the oars as we left the dock that one of them snapped in two. A few minutes later, newer oars in place, Howard pulled us gently away. We picked up speed, however, as his confidence in the strength of the oars grew. Soon it seemed that he had us going fast enough to pull a water-skier! I'd never seen such a wake behind a rowboat.

My favorite fishing spot was a half-mile away, about two hundred yards out from a small point. We reached it as quickly as if we'd had a five-horsepower motor on the boat. We dropped anchor, baited our hooks, and started to fish.

One of the best (or worst) things about fishing with another person is the time it gives you to talk. If your partner is an interesting person, it can be a very rich experience. Imagine having Howard Hummer all to yourself for two hours! We started out with fishing talk—you know, things like how to bait a hook, where to place it (close to the bottom? halfway?), how to make it look alive, how big a fish I caught right here last time, the biggest fish Howard ever caught, what it's like to deep-water fish off the coast of Cape Cod. Then we got into personal things, and I told him about Dad leaving us years ago.

"Are your parents divorced?" he asked.

"No. We've never heard from Dad since he left. Mother doesn't even know if he's still alive."

"I see," Howard nodded his head thoughtfully.

"Reverend Hummer?" I was ready to ask a big question.

"Call me Howard," he said.

"Thanks. Howard, how come there's so much divorce these days? I mean, it seems I'm hearing more and more about it all the time. Why don't marriages last?" Before he could respond, I continued, "You're a pastor, so you marry people, right? Before they marry, do they ever say they expect to divorce someday?"

"Good questions, son. Let me take a crack at answering that last one first."

Just then my line snapped down against the side of the boat. "Got a bite," I shouted. And for the next three minutes I was occupied with reeling the fish into the boat. It was a beautiful bass, a keeper. I attached it to the stringer, rebaited my hook, and put it over the side. Howard began speaking again.

"You know, pastoring is a very interesting job, because you get to know people in every kind of situation. You're there when a baby is born; you're there when his grandparent dies; you oversee the child's religious education; you counsel him through the teenage years; you see him before he falls in love, after he falls in love, before the wedding, after the wedding—and, unfortunately, you're often there after the divorce. I could write a book on what I've heard from divorced people on why their marriage failed."

"Is every story different? Or do they all have similar characteristics?" I asked.

"Every story is different, and they all have similar characteristics. But I don't think marriages fail because of factors such as incompatibility, unfaithfulness, money problems, or just simple boredom, which are so often given as reasons for the failure. These are just symptoms of a deeper problem. In almost every divorce I've known there were two key ingredients that, in my estimation, caused the marriage to fail."

"What were they?" I asked.

"Immaturity and lack of vision." Snap! Snap! One after the other our fishing rods bent. This time it took longer to get the fish to the boat.

"Man! Mine must weigh a ton," I said, straining at my reel.

"Mine too! Boy, this one sure feels funny. If I didn't know better I'd say it was a log or a clump of weeds, but it's got life. Strange play, though." Then at the same time, our rods bent almost double.

"I'm snagged," I said.

"Me too," said Howard. "What in the world's goin' on?" he exclaimed, looking down into the water. Suddenly he laughed. "Ah! There's the problem. I'm snagged on the anchor rope."

"So am I," I laughed too.

"Wait a minute! There's a fish down there."

"Where?"

"Right beside the rope. My fish has wrapped the line around the rope. Where's your fish?"

"That's my fish! Where's yours?"

"No. It's mine. Hold on," he said, his eyes wide with surprise, "I can't believe it—we've caught the same fish!"

He quickly gave me his fishing rod to hold while he pulled up the anchor. Sure enough! There was one fish, and *both* our lines were attached to it! The mystery was solved in a moment.

"Well, look at this," Howard chuckled. "He took your bait and swam away; you jerked your line; and he crossed my line, entangled the two, and then wrapped everything around the anchor rope. Amazing! I've never heard of this one before!"

"Me either," I laughed. "So it's my catch, right?"

"Yep. Score's two to zip," he said with mock disappointment. "But that's a fish story to end all fish stories!" And we had a great laugh together. This was fun. It took a few minutes to settle down, but once our lines were back in the water, he took up where he'd left off.

"When I say 'immaturity' I'm not criticizing anyone for being young. It's just that when you're young you're inexperienced, enthusiastic, and quite selfish. Most of your life to that point has been a process of being cared for and served by parents. Your big struggles have not been adult struggles—like putting food on the table and paying bills. Rather, your focus has been on being liked and how you look. You spend more time in front of a mirror than you do behind a desk or on an assembly line. Your dreams and your talk are about finding a true love, while your parents have been struggling at making a true love last. You tend to be overly sensitive, to overact, and to over-react. So, put the two of you together, and what have you got? An explosion looking for a place to happen."

"I hear what you're sayin'," I responded thoughtfully. "What do you mean by 'vision'?"

"Lack of vision is what I said. Lack of vision. The best way to explain it is to use an illustration," he said, sounding a bit like he was preaching a sermon. "I remember visiting a church summer camp when I was seventeen. It was built on the shores of Lake Ontario and was a small camp, with maybe thirty cottages built along the shoreline. The year I was there, they were opening twenty more lots down at the east end of the camp. Whereas the established cottages were surrounded by rolling lawns and gorgeous mature trees, these east lots were flat and treeless. They looked positively unattractive. But, to my surprise, they were bought up within a week. I couldn't believe it.

"Today they're absolutely beautiful, with lush lawns, full-grown trees, and a developed shoreline. You see, I lacked vision. I didn't see what they could become, given commitment, cultivation, and time. I thought that their condition 'now' would be their condition 'then.' I didn't realize that their potential was as great as the dreams of those who bought them. By the way, there are one or two cottages along that stretch that are overgrown, seedy, and an eyesore. The original owners had vision; but for whatever reason, they had to sell. The next owners lacked vision, or were lazy, or both. A vision has to be cared for."

Howard paused for a few moments, a faraway look in his eye. "You know, there was a time in my life when I lost vision. I saw my life as a wasteland, and there was no goal for me to strive for. I actually thought of ending my life." He paused again, a lump in his throat. "But I was given vision at the last minute." He looked up at me and saw something in my eyes. "You know about Napoleon, don't you?"

"Yes, sir." My throat suddenly felt thick.

"Vision gives you a reason to live and discipline for living. Many of those who divorce have lost sight of the far horizon." We fished for the next half-hour in total silence. Then Howard checked his watch and said, "Guess it's time to go back. Why don't you put on a spinner and troll while I row?"

I did so, and I caught two pike on the way. But my delight at the catch was somewhat muted by what I'd heard. I determined that when it came my turn, I'd think of my wife before myself, and I'd dream a big dream about what our marriage would be. I also determined that I'd follow through and not give up prematurely. And you know what? It worked, and it's working. I credit a lot of the success of our marriage to seeing it as a lifelong commitment. If, on the other hand, I had seen it as a short-term experiment, and had married with "the back door open," chances are I would have used the door.

When we got back to Rainbow Village, David was waiting for us on the dock with an impatient but happy look on his face. "I thought you'd *never* get here," he said, with a mix of exasperation and excitement in his voice. "I want to give you your birthday present, Dad."

He looked at me and said, "Dad turns sixty-five tomorrow. Big birthday, right?" Then, turning back to his father, he said, "Your present is in the truck." He led us to the truck, walking very quickly and occasionally turning back to wait for us, very much like a dog who is trying to get you to hurry up when you're out with him for a walk. When we reached the truck David was already reaching into the front seat. His head still in the cab, he shouted, "Close your eyes!" Both of us obeyed. We heard a little whimper as David said in triumph, "Okay! Open them!" We opened our eyes, and there was a healthy little black Labrador pup. "I got him in Gore Bay," he said as he handed the pup to his father. "What are you going to call him?"

Howard chuckled as the little fellow snuggled under his chin. "How about Napoleon? Yes, Napoleon will do." With that, he turned away from us to look at the lake. All I could see was a little black face nuzzling the lion's ear.

Well, it's time to hit the sack. Aunt Jenny sends her love.

Love you two!
Uncle Bob

33

Dear Jess and Kate,

Hi! How's it going? Boy, were we ever impressed by the news about your BMX Motocross trophy, Kate! I didn't know that those bikes your mom bought with the money we sent were BMXers. And you, Jess, came in fourth in your division? Great stuff! We sure are proud of you two! And, speaking of bikes, it's time to continue that story about my first bike. Mind you, as you'll see, I wasn't exactly in your league. Instead of riding around and over things, I usually ran *into* them! But it's a great story.

Before I get into it, however, I want to talk for a bit about sunglasses. Sunglasses? Yep. Sunglasses.

When I was just five years old, I found a pair of sunglasses in the ditch outside our house. The frames were made of pink plastic and, get this, were *heart*-shaped! I was old enough to realize that they were designed for a girl to wear, but I didn't care. The plastic lenses were so dark that they were almost black. I was amazed at how the world changed when I put them on.

Looking through those lenses blackened the world. The sun could be shining brightly, the trees green and blowing in the wind, the sky a brilliant blue. The children playing in the field could be wearing all shades of red, blue, yellow, and brown. But when I had those glasses on, everything looked either black or gray, almost as if a color television suddenly turned to black and white. Those glasses made a huge difference in how I saw things.

Part of the change had nothing to do with color. Each lens had a deep scratch that was probably the result of the sunglasses falling out of a car and sliding over the gravel road into our ditch. These scratches distorted everything. They didn't make me see double, but they *did* make me see one and a half! What I mean is this: when I looked at a tree, I saw the tree itself and then about half of the same tree spilling out of the edges of the tree trunk. Or I'd look someone in the face, and they'd have three eyes! Or I'd look at a bicycle, and it would have three wheels. It was a riot! If I wore them for more than a few minutes, I'd really start to get confused. With those sunglasses on, the world was a black, gray, and distorted place. When I took them off, everything became colorful again.

What do sunglasses have to do with the story of my first bike? A lot. Keep reading!

Remember that vicious winter storm, and Terry Hale's visit, and the beautiful red bike he showed me in the catalog? Well, I remembered it all too clearly over the next few months. Every night I went to sleep dreaming about that bike. I even cut the page out of the catalog and pinned it to the wall of the bedroom. I woke up thinking about it, and my daydreams at school were full of red paint, chrome wheels, whitewall tires, tan saddles, and pinstriped fenders. I ate and drank that bike. But way down deep I knew I'd never get it. We were just too poor.

There were times when I resented our poverty. I'd look at the picture of the bike on the wall and feel bitter that the world was so unfair. Remembering Roddy Thornton and his room full of toys made me angry. I would think black thoughts and imagine Roddy dead. No kidding. There were times when I hated him that much. And the day Terry Hale rode his new bike into town and came to show it to me, I hit the lowest point of my bitterness and self-pity. Even as he stood beside those gleaming rims and that luscious brown saddle, I had to fight the urge to kick his spokes in. I was mad at him for showing off, at Mother for being so poor, and at my absent dad for making her poor. I was ticked off at everyone.

Strangely, when I was in these dark moods, I thought everyone was against me. I thought the kids at school were making fun of my much-mended clothes, and the teachers were picking on me because I was poor. I snapped at my friends. Not surprisingly, they snapped back, and I took it personally. I brought this blackness home, of course, and made life miserable for Mother, your mom, and myself. And when Mother would object to my mood, I'd bring up the subject of the bike and cruelly hurt her by reminding her that she couldn't buy it for me. I remember catching her at a weak moment once. At the mention of the bike, her face grew white, then gray, and her eyes swelled with tears. I realized I'd overdone it and felt like a rat. But only for a moment. I went to my bed, saw that picture on the wall, and slugged my pillow in anger. The world was black, my life was black, and so was my heart.

That night as I lay in bed, contemplating Terry Hale's slow, agonizing death, I heard your mom stir in her bed across the room.

"Bobby?" she asked, her voice searching for me in the darkness. "Bobby? Are you awake?"

"Yes," I said, a note of impatience in my voice. "Whaddya want?"

"I'm sorry you can't get that bike. If I had the money, I'd buy it for you."

"Sure. *If* you had the money! Well, forget it, Sis, we don't have it and never will," I almost shouted.

"Bobby?"

"What!" I answered, anger in my voice.

"I'd like a bike too."

It's a good thing it was dark. Your mom's words pierced me like a knife, and I'm sure my face would have shown the shock. I'd never thought about *her*—*she* wanted a bike too! She dreamed about a bike too! But there was no bitterness in her voice, no blame in her words. Instead, she was sorry for *me* and would buy one for *me* if she could. A sharp pain pierced my throat, and my eyes filled with hot tears. I buried my face in the pillow and cried silently.

"Bobby? Bobby? Are you awake?"

I didn't answer. I'd never been more miserable in my life. Besides, I was too choked up to talk.

The next morning I was quiet and embarrassed. Mother noticed the change and asked me what was wrong. Instead of scolding me and giving me what I deserved, here she was sympathizing with me. In an awkward and slightly tearful way, I apologized for my foul behavior. I'd hardly gotten the words out of my mouth when she gave me a huge hug and said, "Oh, Bobby. You're so sweet, and such a good boy. I *do* wish I could get you that bike." Then she began to cry. Well, if I had been miserable the night before, I was absolutely at rock bottom now. I tried to comfort her. When she stopped crying, I left for school.

As I walked I noticed that the world had changed. The sun was shining, the sky was blue, the trees were green, and my schoolmates were suddenly cheerful and friendly. Then, as Terry Hale waved at me from across the schoolyard, it hit me—the world hadn't changed at all. *I* had changed. All because of my sweet sister. She had knocked those black, scratched sunglasses off my eyes.

There's much more to poverty than we sometimes think. It can become not just a fact of life, but a way of thinking. It can throw your world into a colorless, black night. You see everything in terms of what you don't have, and you begin to think of yourself as the lowest of the low and the most unlovable, disagreeable, and lonely person on earth. You begin to lose hope of ever rising above or beyond your poverty, and you become angry. The anger, of course, just makes your condition worse. It drives people away and heightens your feelings of envy and bitterness. It's as though you've put on dark, scratched glasses, and your whole world is black and distorted. Poverty is a great evil when it becomes a way of seeing things.

The only way to avoid this is to be thankful. "Thankful? For what?" Well, thankful for legs that can walk, eyes that can see, a place to live, and a school to attend. Thankful that you live in a country where you at least have the freedom to look at that bottle of pop and say, "Hey! That bottle's not half-empty, it's half-full!" Thankful that you have at least one parent at home and that you have a future. Just remember this: 99.9 percent of all the people who have ever lived on this planet have not had the money they needed or wanted. But millions have risen to greatness. How? By the force of money? No. By the force of will.

Speaking of force, I'd better force myself to bring this letter to an end. I could go on and on! But this story of the bike needs at least one more letter. Please forgive me for stretching it out this way. I don't really mean to—it's just that sometimes I get sidelined by things like sunglasses!

I'm looking forward to your letters. Aunt Jenny sends her love. Me too.

Uncle Bob

34

Dear Jess and Kate,

Aunt Jenny and I went to a local baseball game last night. It was a playoff game that went into extra innings. The final score was three to two. But we're still chuckling at what happened, not on the field, but in the stands.

The game had just started when we realized we were going to have an entertaining night. Seated directly in front of us was a very small, excited, and active woman who had a *very* loud voice. In the top of the first inning, when the pitcher retired the first three batters in a row, she jumped up and down after each out, flailing her arms, shouting, "Yes! Yes! Yes! Yes! Yes!" in a voice that would carry a mile over open water.

Then, when the same thing happened in the bottom of the first (only this time it was the visiting team's pitcher who retired all three batters in order), she did it again. "Yes! Yes! Yes! Yes! Yes!" Her body jumped, her arms windmilled, and her voice split the ears of everyone within ten rows of her vocal chords. This pattern continued inning after inning in what was proving to be a real pitchers' duel. There were moments of peace, however. Whenever one or the other pitcher pitched to the opposing pitcher at bat, she would cover her eyes, sink in her seat, and moan. I leaned forward to hear what she was moaning. All I heard was a muffled, jaw-clenched, "No! No! No!"

At the end of nine innings the game was tied 2–2. This was when our schizophrenic fan really got weird. In the top of the tenth, she turned right around and knelt at her seat—no kidding! We heard her moaning, "Oh, God," and groaning, "Please, God!" Her head was buried in her arms, and she appeared to be trying to hide. There were two hits in that inning; and each time as the crowd roared, she put her hands over her ears and pushed her face flat against the seat. No runs scored, however; and as the teams switched field, she came up for air, checked the scoreboard to see what had happened, and knelt at her chair again when play resumed. Then, in the bottom of the tenth, with two out and the count three balls and two strikes on the third batter, there was a mighty crack of the bat, and it was all over—a home run. The crowd went wild as the home team celebrated its victory.

But while everyone seemed to be dancing in the stands, our kneeling fan stood, her face drained of its color. Excusing herself, she made her way out to the aisle muttering, "I *hate* baseball!" Aunt Jenny and I were speechless.

The mystery was solved a moment later when a fan beside us turned and said, "Quite a show, huh?" meaning the woman, not the game.

"That's for sure," I answered. "I've never seen such strange behavior at a game before."

"Oh, she's always like this when her husband and son pitch against each other," he laughed. So that was it! For this poor woman, the game had been an agony of divided loyalties.

Unfortunately, this is the way it is for a lot of kids whose parents divorce. They feel totally torn. They love both parents, want to be with both, and want both to be happy. They've got a huge problem, though. They themselves are happiest when their parents are together, but that seems to be when their parents are the most miserable. Then the problem gets even bigger when the custody battle starts.

A friend of mine, who went through the experience as a kid, described it this way:

In my case, neither of my parents was abusive to me, so I had no reason to dislike either one. What's more, they kept their differences from me. I never heard them fighting, although I often felt the "ice" around our home, especially at mealtime. When my dad's absences increased, I believed my mom when she said it was because of his work. I don't know if she believed it herself, or whether she was trying to convince herself that his work was the problem. As I look back at it, I think she did suspect something, because I saw her going very carefully through the telephone bill once, calling some of the numbers she didn't recognize. I also heard her being very terse one day with some woman who called.

As time went on, my dad started to show a keen interest in me when he *was* at home. He started taking me to ball games, movies, and restaurants. He bought me a new bike, a baseball glove, and new clothes. I loved all this, of course, but I saw that Mom resented it. She didn't seem to have the money he did. But she *did* start treating me with extra care. I loved that too. In fact, I was becoming spoiled when my world fell apart.

It was the first Saturday morning in months that we had sat down at the breakfast table together. Mom had really outdone herself. There were frilly new place mats, a centerpiece of fresh-cut flowers, a fresh coffee cake, and fresh-squeezed orange juice, to accompany a huge breakfast of bacon and eggs. It was all so unusual (Mom was *not* a morning person, and Saturdays were usually sleeping-in days for her) that it almost appeared artificial.

They were both unusually animated that morning. Dad gave me a playful cuff and tousled my hair as he sat down at the table, and Mom made a great fuss over me, seeming very concerned that the coffee was hot enough for Dad's taste. Her waiting on us was so exact and intense that I felt like I was being served at some expensive restaurant. After we'd finished eating—a meal, by the way, full of unusual enthusiasm for small talk—Dad pushed his chair back from the table, leaned forward, and said, "Son, there's something your mother and I need to tell you."

After all these years, I could see the emotion on my friend's face as he recounted what happened next. He cleared his throat and said,

It was as if a dark curtain had suddenly been dropped over a colorful, artificially lit stage. Dad's face turned gray, and Mom's turned a ghostly white. Dad's hands were clasping and unclasping his juice glass, while Mom kept hers folded in her lap, her head down and lips tight, as if she were being scolded by a schoolteacher. Dad then began a tiresome account of how people fall in love and then fall out of love. He was going on and on about how this happened all the time. He said that just because you didn't love someone anymore, that didn't mean you couldn't be friends. I interrupted and blurted, "You're getting divorced, aren't you!"

Mom spoke for the first time. "That's right, son. Your father has a girlfriend and wants to marry her," she said, a tremor of emotion in her voice. "It's been going on for a year."

I looked at Dad for confirmation of this accusation. He just shrugged his shoulders and said, "It's perfectly normal. It happens all the time." At this point Mom exploded. I was suddenly in the middle of a terrible fight. The air was full of charges, counter-charges, and spiteful put-downs. I could hardly believe it. It was like a bad dream.

Then, when things had calmed down a bit, Dad told me that he and Mom had agreed that, since I was twelve years old, I could decide who I'd live with. They said they would leave it entirely up to me and respect my decision. They said I didn't have to decide now, but they'd want an answer in a week or so.

Now all the new stuff and extra care made sense. I got this queasy feeling that my parents, my *own* parents, had been trying to buy me off! Was it because both thought they loved me more than the other, or was it that my living with one would give him or her the status of the better parent? Frankly, my first thoughts that night were angry. I was ticked at both of them. I thought the best thing to do would be to run away. Maybe I'd get hit by a car or die of starvation. Then they'd be sorry. It would serve them right.

Now, I know a lot of kids in my position feel guilt about the divorce, as if it's their fault. Not me. I felt no guilt at all. As far as I was concerned, it was my dad who was guilty—although he said it was Mom's coldness that drove him to it. Still, I laid the guilt at his door. But that didn't make my big decision any easier. I loved them both, and I was terribly torn.

The big problem for me, after I accepted that the whole situation wasn't a bad dream, was my inability to distinguish choosing from rejecting. If I chose Mom I was rejecting Dad, and vice versa. I was leaning more and more toward choosing Mom because it was Dad who was leaving, not her. But I didn't want Dad to think I didn't love him. It was awful.

The issue was decided for me. Not that someone else made the decision. But one day I was downtown on an errand for Mom when I saw a beautiful, brand-new sports car parked across the street. I was standing there, admiring it at a distance, when I saw a happy couple come bouncing out of the restaurant, hand in hand. As the man opened the door of the sports car to let the woman in, I suddenly recognized who he was. He was my dad. I watched them drive away, laughing and obviously in love. I gulped back the stinging tears and the searing pain in my throat and ran home. I burst in the door and announced, "I'm staying with you, Mom." A few days later, when Dad showed up and told me he had a new car, I didn't even go out to take a look. "I thought you loved Corvettes," he said, disappointment in his eyes.

"I *do* love Corvettes," I answered bitterly, "but I don't like yours!" I could see the hurt on his face, but I didn't care. I was glad. At least, I was sort of glad, until that night. When I went

to bed, a deep sense of loss overwhelmed me, and I cried myself to sleep.

He looked at me, and his eyes filled with tears. He said, "You
know, it's been twenty-five years since I refused to ride in that car.
He still has it. He married and divorced two more times. But he
still has that Corvette." Then he paused and said, "And in a
strange sort of way, he still has a part of my heart."

Divided loyalties. They can tear your heart into pieces. Like
the woman at the ball game, you find your heart crying yes and
no at the same time. If my friend's example is any indication of
the norm, chances are you'll feel this conflict, to a greater or lesser
degree, for the rest of your lives.

I have no ready answers to what must be a very powerful
conflict in your hearts. I know you love your dad, even though
he's gone. And I know you sometimes wonder if you might have
been happier with him. Just remember that none of us knows
"what might have been," and we never will. We've got to deal
with what is.

There *is* one thing you can do, however. You can decide *now*
that you will approach marriage with a commitment to make it
last. You can break the mold. Yours can be a lifelong relationship.
It all depends on you.

Looking forward to your letters!

All my love,
Uncle Bob

35 ✍️

Dear Jess and Kate,

Hi. How *are* you? Thanks for the pictures of those *huge* fish you caught last summer, Kate. It reminded me of Howard Hummer, my fishing mate.

A few days after his dad's birthday, David Hummer dropped by Rainbow Village again. I was just walking up from the dock when I saw his truck drive in. I ran up as he brought it to a halt.

"How ya doin'?" he said as he jumped out.

"Great," I answered. "How's Napoleon?"

"Super. He and Dad are getting along just fine. Dad's already had him swimming in Lake Mindemoya. He *loves* it!"

"Isn't he a bit young for that?"

"For sure. But Dad carries him in and holds his hands cupped around Napoleon's little body and gently immerses him. You should have seen him the first time! Napoleon knew what to do immediately. There was Dad holdin' him around the middle, and his little legs were paddlin' to beat the band! He's a natural."

I could imagine huge Howard Hummer and tiny Napoleon playing in the water together. What a sight that must have been. But none of us could imagine that Napoleon would live for a vigorous, joyful twenty years as Howard's closest companion. It was the beginning of a beautiful friendship.

And, as the years went by, what a swimmer Napoleon became! He was the most fearless of dogs. He would jump into the water on any day, at any place, at any time. He was best known, however, for swimming *underwater*. Many times the islanders would see Napoleon run into a lake or jump off a dock, disappear, and, like a loon, reappear several yards from where he'd submerged. He used to go down a fair distance and retrieve things

167

that were sitting on the bottom—logs, stones, keys, wallets, you name it. Once he appeared from one of these underwater swims with a fish in his jaws! But his fame was forever established the time he dove in after a toddler who had fallen off the government dock on Lake Kagawong.

It happened to be a stormy day, and the child's mom, who was a poor swimmer, had failed in her desperate attempts to rescue her drowning son. Howard and Napoleon happened to be driving along as she madly ran up to the road and flagged them down. In a moment they were on the dock. Howard gave a hand signal, and Napoleon plunged into the water. About twenty anxious seconds later he reemerged, the child firmly but gently in his massive jaws. Howard lifted him onto the dock and administered artificial respiration, and the boy lived. The mother, beside herself with worry one moment and deliriously grateful the next, told the story to the local newspaper. Within days Napoleon was the most famous dog in the history of the island. Both the prime minister of Canada and the president of the United States sent letters of commendation.

There was another rescue that would have made him almost as famous, except that he already *was* famous. Let's just say it elevated him from hero to legend.

This is a story of Napoleon, a fawn, and a fox. Before I can tell you what happened, I need to give you some background. First, let me tell you about the fox.

One spring the farmers who lived in the Gore Bay area began to lose a lot of chickens. They quickly concluded that the culprit was the fox who seemed to be appearing every day, running through their fields, across the roads, and in the ditches. The fox was acting erratically, and its frequent appearances near houses and barns led the farmers to believe that it was rabid. Rabies, as you may know, is a very serious disease that almost always causes death.

Foxes are often victims of rabies, perhaps catching it from small animals like skunks who are infected. Its name is taken from an old Latin word that means "rage" or "fury." It's an appropriate name, because infected animals often become wildly aggressive, attacking anything in their way. They also tend to foam at the mouth. That's because rabies victims can't swallow water. So the combination of frenzied behavior with advancing dehydration quickly reduces the victim to a panting, painful death. The big fear, of course, is of being bitten by a rabid animal. Rabies in humans can be cured, but it can be painful and needs to be treated as soon as possible. This is why the Gore Bay farmers all brought out their 22-caliber rifles. They wanted this fox dead.

At this time other animals were appearing in the farmers' fields, especially at dusk. They were herds of deer. Sometimes, if you were driving down one of the secondary roads in the Gore Bay area, you'd see as many as twenty deer at one time, feeding in the fields. Some of the does had small, frisky fawns at their side. One early evening something unusual and tragic happened. The man who saw it, a farmer named Fred Thurmon, described the event this way:

"I was drivin' down Harrison's side road there, behind this delivery truck from Little Current, when I sees this commotion in Erickson's field. There's this herd of deer scatterin' here and there, and this fox is after 'em. Strange to see a fox after deer, eh? Well, anyway, this one doe and her fawn comes runnin' our way. The guy in the truck, I don't think he even was watchin'. Before you know it, the doe, she's spooked right in front of the truck and he hits her head-on, knockin' her flyin'. He didn't even stop. I stops, and there's the doe lyin' dead by the road, and the fawn, all confused and scared, is standin' beside her, bleatin' like a sheep. I didn't know what to do. Thought maybe I'd capture the fawn so's the wife could feed it an' all, but soon's I try to get near it, it takes off into the field—poor little critter. Never thought I'd hear tell of it again."

The very next day David and Howard Hummer, with Napoleon in the back of the pick-up, drove to Gore Bay. Napoleon loved riding in the back. He'd stand on his rear legs, his front legs on the cab of the truck, the wind blowing his ears straight back, and his lips pushed back from his teeth by the turbulence. This full-toothed smile made him look a bit crazy. Add to that his attempts to snag insects, butterflies, and a reckless bird or two with his mouth as David drove, and you've got quite a scene. Some people nearly drove off the road watching this strange sight. Napoleon didn't care. He loved it and used to bark wildly as they bounced along.

Howard had been living with David in Mindemoya for a couple of years already, and the pile of firewood he had chopped was already causing comment among the islanders. He liked to buy his wood-chopping equipment at the hardware store in Gore Bay. That morning's trip was for this very purpose.

Gore Bay was (and is) a peaceful little town on the northern shore of Manitoulin Island. Its main street was lined with shops, and at the far end it led to a beautiful little natural harbor. Every summer it swelled with visiting sailboats from as far away as the Florida Keys. Even though the sailing season hadn't officially begun, several sailboats were tied to the docks as the Hummers rolled into town. They pulled up in front of the hardware store just as it happened.

Without warning a frightened fawn appeared, running for its life down the middle of the street. Close behind was a wild-eyed fox. Everyone was so shocked by the suddenness of it all that they seemed rooted to the spot. But not Napoleon. He leaped out of the truck and took up the chase even as David, Howard, and several others found their feet and began running too. The fawn darted here and there in her flight, but very quickly turned toward the harbor at the end of the street. She hesitated momentarily as she saw the water and the sailboats. Her indecision lasted only a second or two, but that was enough time for the fox to throw itself at the fawn's hindquarters. He grabbed hold of her left rear leg and pulled her down. That would have been it, except for a black blur that threw itself on the fox. Napoleon had arrived. He sank his teeth into the fox's neck and lifted and shook him violently back and forth. After two or three of these snaps the fox's neck broke, and he hung limply in Napoleon's jaws.

Meanwhile, the fawn picked herself up and ran blindly toward the docks. Again she stopped, caught between the town and the water. She made a motion as if she were going to run back into town, when David and Howard and several others came running to the scene. In desperation the fawn jumped onto the dock and then up onto one of the sailboats. Her feet splayed, she lost her balance, and she fell with a splash into the water. She went under but came up a few moments later and began swimming out into the harbor. She was really struggling, and it was plain to all who watched that in a minute or two she would drown.

Howard quickly assessed the situation and ordered Napoleon to let go of the fox. This was the only time in their twenty-year relationship that Napoleon would ever hesitate before obeying Howard. He was proud of his kill and didn't want to let it go. Howard shook his finger at Napoleon and, in a loud voice, gave the order a second time. Even as Napoleon let go, Howard gave him the order to jump in the water and retrieve.

Napoleon leaped to obey. He knew that saving the fawn was his goal, not killing her. By this time the fawn was about one hundred feet from shore and beginning to take in water. The people could hear her gasping and coughing as she swam, terrified. Napoleon, however, swam with awesome confidence and strength. His large head and broad shoulders pumped powerfully as he stroked his way toward the drowning fawn. When he was about twenty feet away she went down. To the amazement of those watching who didn't know Napoleon's reputation, so did he! About thirty seconds later he reappeared, his vicelike jaws gently enclosing the unconscious fawn's neck. In no time he was back on shore and deposited the limp form of the tiny deer at Howard's feet.

Now, it just so happened that the district veterinarian, Douglas Stark, had his office in the building next to the harbor. He had run out to see what was going on and very quickly took charge of the fawn. He bent over her and, after listening carefully at her mouth, he declared that she was still alive. Someone produced a blanket, and Dr. Stark wrapped the fawn in it and carried her to his clinic. As he did so he called Howard over.

"The fawn's going to make it, but we're going to have to put your dog in quarantine," he said.

"Quarantine? How come?" Howard said, shocked.

"Just in case that fox had rabies. I'll send it to the lab for tests. It'll be at least two or three days before we have the results."

Howard was devastated. It would be hard enough to imprison Napoleon in a strange kennel for a few days. But what if that fox was rabid? It meant that Napoleon would have to be put to sleep—forever.

For the next two days and nights Howard stayed beside Napoleon's kennel. For his part, Napoleon took it quite well, although he was a bit confused by this turn of events. But in the end it all worked out well.

On the third day Dr. Stark came into the room containing Napoleon's kennel and announced, "Well, Howard, you can let him out! No rabies."

"Oh, thank God," Howard exclaimed. He opened the kennel, and Napoleon smothered him with doggy kisses.

"Wasn't rabies at all. That poor fox had been shot, maybe months ago. The bullet lodged in his spine. He must have been in constant, excruciating pain. Probably drove him crazy," Dr. Stark said. "So what do you think of your dog, Howard? I'll tell you what the people think—they think he's almost human. Quite the hero. Yep. Quite the hero," he said, as he patted Napoleon's head and went out. Napoleon just wagged his tail and grinned. He caught two butterflies on his way home.

Sometimes, Jess and Kate, you're going to feel just like that fawn—scared and going down. Your dad's absence will sometimes leave you feeling abandoned and alone. But I want you to know that at some of the most critical moments, help will arrive from unexpected sources. Be prepared to be surprised.

And always remember that you're loved. By your mom and by Aunt Jenny and me. You're going to make it!

Love you,
Uncle Bob

36 _____ ✍

Dear Jess and Kate,

Okay. The P.S. in your last letter made the point. You have my word. I promise that the story of my first bike will be complete when this letter ends. There'll be nothing left to say. You'll have every juicy detail. Okay? Okay. It's a promise.

Even though I had taken off those dark glasses of self-pity, making the world bright again, I still wanted a bike. Spring was in full bloom, and it seemed every kid in town was riding a bicycle. I'd watch them riding by, especially on a sunny Saturday or Sunday, and die with longing. But I'd learned not to be bitter about it, so I just kind of ached inside. I caught Mother looking at me during one of my "achey" moments, a look of deep love and concern on her face. Without saying a word she put her arm around my shoulder and sighed. I squeezed her arm and said, "It's okay, Mother, I don't really need one—really." Her eyes told me she appreciated my generous words, but she didn't believe them. She clenched her jaw a few times and then said the strangest thing. "If you had a bike, Bobby, would you know how to ride it?"

"Sure! No sweat. It's easy to ride a bike," I answered, a sudden knot in my stomach. I was caught between two totally unexpected feelings. One was the glimmer of hope in Mother's question, "If you had a bike . . ." (could it be possible she was actually going to get me one?). The second was the troubling awareness that as much as I wanted one, I'd never ridden one. I didn't know how to ride a bike! I had a moment of panic, and the blood drained from my face. Just then Molly Sandstrom went riding past our house on her bicycle. A wild idea hit me. I gave Mother a quick kiss on the cheek and went running out the front door, calling loudly after Molly.

There must have been a note of desperation in my voice, because she slammed the brakes on immediately. I sprinted up to her and, in a breathless voice, asked if she would teach me how to ride. With a startled look she asked, "Here?"

"No, not here." I puffed. "In the back alley." Even though I was swept away with excitement, I still had my pride. I didn't want any guys seeing me riding a *girl's* bike, let alone falling off (as I was sure would happen).

I think Molly was a bit flattered by this unexpected request and answered immediately, "Sure! Let's go!" So we crossed the road and went to the alleyway behind her house.

"It's really easy," she said as she stood beside her bike. "You just hold tightly on to the handlebars and put your leg through here." (In those days girls' bikes had no crossbar. Instead, they had a double frame swooping down from the handlebars to the pedals and then up to the seat.) "Put your foot on one pedal, and pu-u-u-sh off . . . like this!" And she took off in an easy motion.

I ran beside her shouting, "Okay! Okay! I can do it. Let me try!" I was impatient to get at it.

"All right, Bobby, all right," she said, braking to a stop and handing the bike to me. "Just do what I did and you'll be fine."

I gripped the handlebars, swung my leg through, put my right foot on the pedal, and pushed off with my left. I immediately lost my balance, but managed to get my left foot back on the ground to keep the bike upright. I pushed off again, and this time my right foot pushed the pedal toward the ground, increasing my speed. Without any warning the bike lurched to the right, and I crashed. Unfortunately, I fell right on top of the bike, and one of the handlebars speared my stomach, knocking the breath completely out of my lungs. I felt as though the handlebar had gone right through me. I opened my mouth in desperation, trying to draw a breath, and couldn't!

In a panic, I staggered to my feet and started running, doubled over, trying to find a breath somewhere. I could hear Molly screaming at me, but I kept running wildly. My lungs felt like they were on fire, and my stomach felt like it would explode with pain. Then everything went black, and I fell to the ground. The next thing I knew, I was looking up at Molly as she pushed up and down on my chest. With great relief I realized I was breathing. But my stomach was hurting so much that I felt like throwing up. Slowly, however, the pain subsided, and I sat up.

"You okay?" Molly asked, her voice heavy with concern.

"Yeah," I gasped. "But I feel like I've been stabbed." I ran both hands over my stomach, expecting to find a gaping hole. I found only a rip in my shirt.

"You're gonna be all right," said Molly, "I think you just got your wind knocked out. Wanna try the bike again?"

"No way. Not today, anyway," I answered, then picked myself up to go home. Molly walked with me, pushing her bike at her side. When we got to our house, your mom, who was sitting on the front steps reading a book, looked up, smiled, and ran to us, piping cheerfully, "Hey, Molly! Can I take another ride?"

Before Molly could answer, your mom took the bike. Even though it was much too big for her, she pumped eagerly away down the street. I couldn't believe it. "I taught her last week," Molly said, blushing in embarrassment for me. "She picked it up real quick. Must be because she's a girl, and it's a girl's bike and all," she added quietly. I just looked at her wordlessly and went into the house, my face burning with shame.

That evening I said very little over supper and went to bed early. As I drifted to sleep, all I could see was my little sister on Molly's bike, the handlebars at about eye level as she pumped her short legs, riding beautifully down the street. Believe me, the pain of that picture was much greater than the pain radiating from the ugly black and blue bruise on my stomach. I felt totally humiliated.

My feelings didn't improve much the next morning when Mother said over breakfast, "Billy Barber's mother told me yesterday that Billy wants to sell his bike." The oatmeal in my stomach turned to lead. "For only five dollars," she added brightly. "What do you think, Bobby?"

I was struck dumb. I knew that Mother's use of the word *only* to describe the five dollars was brave of her (five dollars bought an entire week's groceries for us) and that I should be gracious in my answer. But I couldn't do anything but look at her as if she'd slapped me. "Billy Barber's bike?" I gasped. "It's a wreck, Mother. It's the ugliest, crummiest bike in town. The pedals are broken, it has no fenders, the frame is bent, it's, it's . . ." I hesitated because of the hurt look on Mother's face. "It's no good, Mother." Then, thinking of what a sacrifice it would be for her to spend five dollars, I added, trying to sound grown up, "It's not worth the money." For some reason this amused her.

"You're really stretching, aren't you, Bobby?" she chuckled.

"No, I'm serious," I said, sounding like I was discussing math grades with my teacher. "It's not worth the money." With desperation overtaking me, I pled, "Please don't buy me Billy's bike! Please!" Then I said something I've regretted ever since. "If Billy Barber's bike is what you're gonna buy me, then I'd rather have no bike at all!" As soon as I said it I knew I shouldn't have. Mother looked like I'd punched her.

I got up from the table and went outside in misery. All my hopes had been dashed. Only yesterday I'd been almost intoxicated with the wild hope that Mother was going to get me a bike. Now, twenty-four hours later, I had no hope of ever getting one. And the black and blue pain in my stomach told me I had no hope of ever riding one. It was one of the lowest points in my young life.

For the next few months I put bicycles out of my mind. I even took the catalog picture of Terry Hale's bike off the wall. In fact, I was almost entirely successful in denying that bikes even existed. But your mom kept bringing me back to reality by riding Molly's bike, her little head bobbing up and down, over and under the oversized handlebars. Then, the day after the summer holidays started, it happened.

I had been sliding the chute all morning and was on my way home for lunch. As I walked I suddenly heard the unmistakable sound of Mr. Martin's dray coming down the street behind me. I turned to look just as Mr. Martin called "Whoa!" and stopped the horses beside me.

"Want a ride, Bobby?" he asked, smiling his huge smile.

"Sure!"

"Hop on!" So I hopped on, he clucked at the horses, and we were off.

"What's a *dray,* Uncle Bob?" I can hear you asking. Well, the best way to describe it is to call it a delivery cart without sides. It was about eight feet wide, twelve feet long, and was pulled by two Clydesdale horses called Pork and Bess. Mr. Martin had customized his dray by putting real airplane wheels and tires on it, which gave it a smooth ride. He often gave us kids rides as he delivered goods around town. It wasn't uncommon to see four or five kids at a time riding along, their feet hanging freely over the sides. Sometimes we'd spend most of the day with Mr. Martin, helping him lift boxes on and off. On this day I was his only passenger, and there was only one box, a fairly large cardboard one, with the name "J. C. Higgins" stamped on it.

"Who are the Higginses?" I asked Mr. Martin. "Do they live around here?"

"Huh? What's that? The Higginses?" he grunted. "Oh. No!" he said, suddenly laughing. "That name on the box is the brand name."

"Brand name?" I asked.

"The name of the manufacturer. You know. The name of the company that made the bike."

"The bike! You mean there's a bike in that box?" My heart started to thump.

"Yep. Sure is. A shiny, new J. C. Higgins bike."

A jolt ran through me, almost as if I'd grabbed hold of an electric wire. Trying to keep the tremor out of my voice, I asked, "Where are you delivering it?"

"Uhmm. Let me check that address again." He reached into his pocket and drew out a crumpled invoice. "Ah, yes. It's goin' to, uh, 17 Ash Street. Do ya know who lives there?"

My heart exploded within me. I looked at him dumbly and could barely squeak out, "I do, Mr. Martin. That's my address."

"I thought so," he chuckled, a twinkle in his eye. "Any idea who the lucky kid is?" I didn't answer because I couldn't talk. I rode the remaining three blocks in a daze.

When we got to our house Mother was outside, working in the garden. She looked up as Mr. Martin pulled on the reins and uttered a loud "Whoa!" to Pork and Bess. Her smile changed to a look of surprise as she saw me stand up on the dray.

"Hi, Mother!" I shouted cheerfully.

"Hello, son," she answered, her eyes darting back and forth from me to Mr. Martin.

"He knows, ma'am," Mr. Martin said with a grin. "Here, Bobby, help me lift it down." At that moment I was torn. Should I jump down, embrace Mother, and shout and dance for joy? Or should I be cool and help Mr. Martin, just as I had done so often before with other boxes? I decided to play it cool, especially because some of the neighborhood kids had started to gather. But I'm sure my actions betrayed me. I was so excited that all my movements were exaggerated. I lifted harder than I had to, I grunted and wheezed harder than the strain demanded, and I was unusually serious, as if I had just committed myself to some death-defying mission. In other words, I was delirious with joy on the inside and cool as a cucumber on the outside. And the tension was almost more than I could bear.

As Mother signed the delivery log, Mr. Martin, who was obviously enjoying playing Santa Claus, said, "It's lunchtime, ma'am. Would you like me to assemble the bike for Bobby?"

"Oh, that would be great, Mr. Martin!" Mother answered, her hand on my trembling shoulder. "I'll go in and get our tool box."

"No need, ma'am. I've some right here on the dray." He quickly got his tools, popped the staples from the box, and began to pull out my bicycle, piece by piece. First came the handlebars, then the shiny chrome wheels. Next came the tires, the tubes still folded into small cardboard containers. After that came the fenders and, finally, the frame. And to my everlasting delight, I realized I was looking at the same bike Terry Hale had shown me in the catalog on that fateful, stormy winter's day. When he pulled out the tan leather saddle with, "By golly! Lookee here. Thought I had everything," I could have cried for joy.

Mr. Martin went to work, and within twenty minutes my new bike stood before me. Quite literally it was the bike of my dreams.

As I saw it there, gleaming in the sun, I lost my cool. My eyes brimmed with tears and I grinned from ear to ear. "Thanks, Mr. Martin," I said as he handed it over to me. Then I turned to Mother. I wanted to say, "Forgive me for being a jerk" or "How did you *do* it?" or "I don't deserve this." But all that came out was, "Thanks, Mother. It's what I always wanted!"

"I know, son. I hope you enjoy it," she responded. Then, in front of all those kids (about eight had gathered around the incredible red machine), she gave me a hug and a kiss.

"So, aren't you going to ride it?"

"Now?" I gasped, not thinking what a dumb thing that was to say.

"Of course, *now*. I didn't buy it for you just to look at."

"That's right!" one of the kids shouted. "C'mon, Bobby, let us see you ride your bike!" I looked at Molly Sandstrom, who'd just joined the group and felt a sudden handlebar-sized pain in my stomach. "C'mon, Bobby! Whatcha waitin' for?"

I was trapped. What could I do? So, as Mr. Martin held the bike steady, I climbed on. Then, with the cheers of my friends drowned out by the pounding of my heart, he gave me a push and I was off! To my astonishment I actually stayed upright for several yards, but I was totally out of control. I drove right off the road and crashed into the ditch. The children were greatly amused by this, laughing and hooting while Mr. Martin picked me up, dusted me off, and put me back on the bike.

"I know you're embarrassed, son" he whispered to me. "But if you don't learn now, you never will." So he gave me another push. This time I went a bit farther, but ended up entangled in the Krauses' hedge. There was more laughter from my friends as Mr. Martin rescued me once more. He put me on the bike, this time running beside me as I began to pedal, his hand on the saddle. I rode like this for several hundred feet, my excitement mounting as I got the feel of it. Then, to my great shock, I heard Mr. Martin calling, "You're doin' great, Bobby! Keep it up!" He'd let go, and I was still riding! I gave a shout of triumph and rode right around the block. My wildest dreams had come true.

That night I insisted on keeping the bike in our bedroom. I'll never forget the joyful feeling I had as I looked at it leaning against the wall where the picture from the catalog used to hang. I was so full of happy feelings and thoughts that my toes were curling. It took me forever to get to sleep. I don't think there was a happier boy on earth. I had only one moment of sober thought: when your mom looked across the room at the bike and said, "Congratulations, Bobby, I'm very happy for you." But there was something in her voice that said, "If only you knew how much I want one too."

The next morning Mother handed me an envelope. She told me it had five dollars in it, and I was to take it to the Sears mail-order office on Main Street. I was glad to do it. Any excuse to ride my bike was welcome.

"Don't forget the receipt," she called after me as I rode off.

"No problem, Mother," I called back, actually turning my head to look at her (without losing my balance!). In minutes I was at the corner of Main and Elm, momentarily shocked at what I was seeing. The entire sidewalk in front of Sears was on fire! It took me a few seconds to figure it out. There were two town trucks with crushed stone in the boxes, two hot tar machines, and several men at work. They were spreading the tar on the sidewalk, lighting it on fire to make it smooth as water, and then spreading crushed stone on the tar to create a surface similar to asphalt. I sat watching this for a while. Then, leaving my bike on its side in the vacant lot, I crossed the street and jumped across the hot sidewalk right into Sears' doorway.

The clerk took the envelope and said, more to herself than to me, "Oh. Here's the first payment on that bike." She then stamped the receipt and gave it to me. I turned to leave, feeling somewhat humbled by the knowledge that Mother was paying five dollars a month for my bike. I jumped across the sidewalk and looked up just as one of those town trucks backed right over my bike. I stood there, rooted to the spot in horror as the truck pulled ahead, crushing my bike again, and then backed up once more, crumpling it beyond repair.

I suddenly found my legs and my voice. I ran over to the truck, shouting at the truck driver, "My bike! My bike! You've run over my bike!" He opened the door, looked down at me and said, "I've done what, kid?"

My face flooded with tears, I sobbed, "You've run over my bike! You've ruined it!" He jumped down and pulled it out from beneath the truck. It was totally destroyed. The frame was bent; both wheels were bent; the fenders were bent. I was heartbroken.

"Sorry, kid," was all the driver said as he climbed back into the truck and drove away. I collapsed to the ground beside my mortally wounded dream machine and wept so violently that my ribs hurt. No one came to comfort me. The workmen kept working, and the shoppers walked right past me. Finally I stood up and started pushing my bike home. The front wheel could still turn, although it rubbed pitifully against the fork. But the rear wheel wouldn't turn at all; the flat tire just scraped along. My eyes and nose flooded over with sorrow, my heart bursting with pain, I dragged my broken dream home to Mother.

Mother has often told me over the years that the saddest thing she's ever seen was me hauling that wrecked bike into the yard. She held and comforted me, and I heard her voice harden with determination as she said, "I'm going over to Mayor Davidson's house right now. The town workers did this, and the town will have to replace it." And you know what? She was right. The town did pay for it.

Within a week Mr. Martin was pulling another bike out of a box and assembling it for me. What's more, after hearing about my tragedy, he'd come over and worked a whole day straightening the bent bike. He did a beautiful job—so much so that it ran just as well as before. And guess who got this restored beauty? You guessed it—your mom!

I want to share one final thought before I close this lengthy letter. Even though life has dealt you a cruel blow in the divorce of your parents, it hasn't dealt you a mortal blow. You're still alive. You've got years ahead of you that will be filled with unexpected joy. Your dream may not come true today. But tomorrow is another day.

I sure love you,
Uncle Bob

37 _____

Dear Jess and Kate,

Your mom called last night and said she'd told you about the man who wants to marry her. I guess you had quite a conversation. I'd really like you to tell me about it in your next letters. It's a very important discussion. That's why I want to respond to what your mom told me on the phone.

First of all, I think it's pretty obvious that change doesn't come easily to any of us, whether we're young or old. Everyone, with very few exceptions, likes to live with the familiar, the comfortable, the known. None of us likes to deal with the unknown. It's scary and makes us feel uncertain and insecure.

That's what makes starting at a new school so difficult. It's bad enough starting a new grade at an old school. But when you have to begin classes at an entirely different location, it's downright nerve-racking. What will the kids be like? What will they think of me? Who will my teacher be? What will he or she be like? Are my clothes cool? Do the kids ride bikes to school, or is that uncool? Do they bring lunches in brown bags, in pails, or in those new designer bags? Are they all rich? Do they carry guns? Will somebody beat me up? Will anybody like me? And these are the questions that arise in just the first minute! Little wonder that you arrive the first day in a state. Perhaps the only comfort is knowing that there probably are several other kids going through the same thing you are.

Second, we all like routine. Each of us has a certain way of doing things, right? And this is true not only day to day, but year to year as well. For instance, Aunt Jenny and I follow the same pattern every Christmas season. It starts right after Thanksgiving. Aunt Jenny will start talking about Christmas trees, and by December 1 she's playing Christmas music on the stereo and shopping for bargains on wrapping paper and tree ornaments. By December 8 she's bought our *first* tree. That's right—*first* tree—we always get two, because the first one dries out before December 25. That night we erect the tree, decorate it (with "O Tannenbaum!" playing in the background), and drink hot apple cider. The last ornament to put on the tree is always the beautiful wax angel with the deep red brocade robe we bought in Rottenburg, Germany, at the Christmas Store, years ago. Then, three weeks later, we do it all over again with a new tree. Crazy, huh? But that's our routine. What's yours?

I'll bet you always sit at the same place at the table every mealtime. You probably have a very predictable Saturday morning routine and a go-to-bed routine ("Mom! It's too early!"). You take the same route to school every day, right? When you think about it, our lives are framed by this kind of predictability. We're creatures of habit.

But then, wham! A while back all your routines were thrown out of whack by your parents' divorce. It seemed that suddenly nothing was for sure, and you didn't know who to believe or who you could trust. Maybe you still feel that way. Nevertheless, since the divorce you've begun to get back into a rhythm again. Life is starting to regain a measure of predictability. You're sleeping better at night, and your marks at school are improving. (I hope!) What were new routines a few months ago are now becoming familiar. Then wham! It happens again.

This time it's a new relationship. Your mom told you about "him." You thought he was just a friend—now she's calling him her boyfriend. Jess, you especially are feeling threatened by this new male in the mix, and I don't blame you. After all, how do you know if he'll treat her well? And how's he going to treat you and Kate? Maybe he won't want you. It's perfectly natural for you to be suspicious and angry. As for you, Kate, I understand how you feel too. No one can, or should, take the place of your dad. He's not perfect, but you love him. And that's the way it should be. So what to do?

Tough question.

Perhaps the toughest answer is that there's not much you *can* do. Not just because you two are children, but also because it's hard for you to see your mom not just as your mom but as a person with needs. Like you, she has a need to be loved, to be held, to be cared for. For you she is a caregiver. For herself she needs to be a caretaker as well.

Although your mom is an adult and probably seems quite old to you, to others her age she is a vital, attractive woman. In fact—hold onto your seats here!—some men see her as very beautiful. Yep. That's right. Very beautiful! She is full of life and has the best part of her life ahead of her. Many men would love to have her as their friend, lover, and wife, for the rest of their lives. Looks like she's narrowed the field, however. (What's his name? Tom?) And—hang on again!—most of her life is going to be lived with him (or someone like him), not you!

No, I'm not suggesting that she's going to leave you. Rather, I'm simply saying that in a few years you're going to leave her. You're growing up real fast. Soon, too soon, you'll be young adults setting out on your own. Believe it or not, when that happens, she'll still have a full life to live.

Please don't think, by the way, that you are a hindrance to your mom's happiness. You *are* her happiness. Only a parent understands how true that statement is. But there is more to your mom than mothering. Inside that adult body is a vital woman with lots of the world and of life to explore. Inside she's still growing, and she will be until she dies. That's why she'll always be a fascinating friend. One day she'll be your peer, not just your parent. But the key thing now for you to do is to give her lots of support and room to grow.

"Support? How do I give Mom support?" I can hear you asking. It's simple. Give her lots of hugs and tell her how much you love her. Do it often. And—here's a tough one—tell her that whatever man she chooses to love, maybe to marry, will be all right with you. If she loves him, you'll love him—eventually! She needs to hear that. It will liberate her. Believe me.

Why? Because the most important people in her life are you two. Tom is becoming important too. But with him she's just now establishing a bond. With you, she has a bond stronger than life itself. That's why she'd die for you if she had to. She *loves* you—big time!

"Okay, Uncle Bob," you may ask, "we hear you. But what about us? What if he doesn't love us? And what about his kids? How are we going to get along with them?" Whew! That's another toughie!

What I'm about to say now, your mom may or may not agree with. At best, I think she'll have mixed feelings. But here goes anyway. If she marries Tom, I don't think you should feel pressured to call him *Dad*. First of all, he's *not* your dad, and secondly, you don't feel like he's your dad. So why fake it? Over time you might see him more and more as a dad. Maybe, maybe not. But for a beginning, call him Tom.

Try to show respect, however. Do this not just for his sake, but for your mom's sake. You can be sure she'll be very sensitive about your reaction. And the question she'll be asked most by friends and relatives will be, "How are Jess and Kate taking it?" What a relief it would be for her to be able to say, "They're doing real well. They're showing great maturity, and I think they're liking him more and more all the time."

And remember this: Tom will need all the support you can give him as well. Can you imagine how he will feel, taking on a new wife and two new kids? He's human too, and probably as scared as can be. He'll want very much to have you like him. And I'll bet he's hoping that one day you might even *love* him. I expect that's his commitment to you, as well—he *will* love you one day. Maybe sooner than later.

"But the kids, Uncle Bob. What about Tom's kids?" Hey, I don't have any answers here. I don't know what they're like. I don't know whether they're young or old, mature or immature, boys or girls. There's one thing I *do* know, however. They're as scared as you are. If there's one thing you can do that will make the situation easier, it's this: reach out to them. Show interest. Be friendly. Make room. Do for them what you'd like them to do for you.

Sure, you're probably going to have your moments. There'll be a few fights and several moments of tears and frustration. But over time—key word: *time*—you'll feel more and more like a family. It'll be a *blended* family, but a family nonetheless. And you know what? I think it'll get better every year.

And get this: I'll be their Uncle Bob too! Scary thought! Aunt Jenny and I love you.

Always,
Uncle Bob

About the Author

James Cantelon is a cohost of "100 Huntley Street" and the host of "Talk to Me," a television talk show broadcast live fifteen hours a week to over thirty million homes. He is a former pastor and the author of *Theology for Non-Theologians*. Cantelon and his family live in Ontario, Canada.